Egyptian Tomb Architecture

The archaeological facts of pharaonic circular symbolism

David I. Lightbody

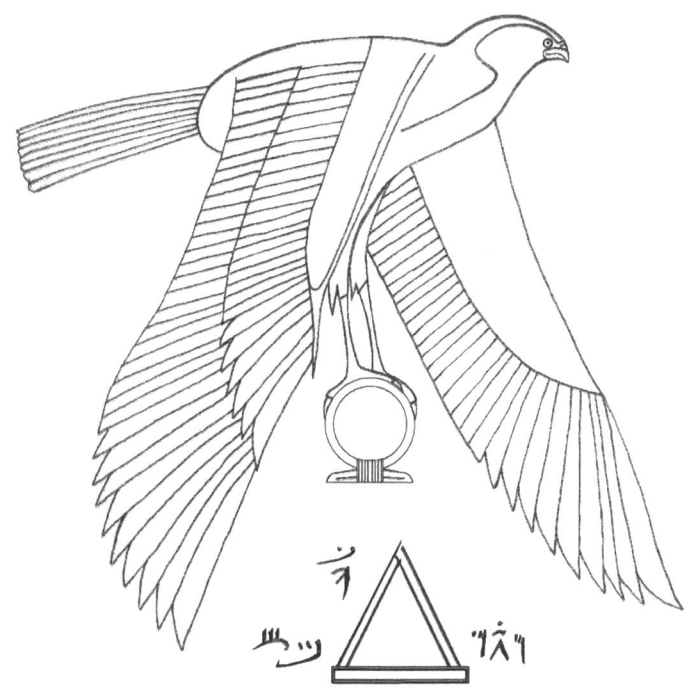

BAR International Series 1852
2008

Published in 2016 by
BAR Publishing, Oxford

BAR International Series 1852

Egyptian Tomb Architecture

ISBN 978 1 4073 0339 0

© D I Lightbody and the Publisher 2008

The author's moral rights under the 1988 UK Copyright,
Designs and Patents Act are hereby expressly asserted.

All rights reserved. No part of this work may be copied, reproduced, stored,
sold, distributed, scanned, saved in any form of digital format or transmitted
in any form digitally, without the written permission of the Publisher.

BAR Publishing is the trading name of British Archaeological Reports (Oxford) Ltd.
British Archaeological Reports was first incorporated in 1974 to publish the BAR
Series, International and British. In 1992 Hadrian Books Ltd became part of the BAR
group. This volume was originally published by Archaeopress in conjunction with
British Archaeological Reports (Oxford) Ltd / Hadrian Books Ltd, the Series principal
publisher, in 2008. This present volume is published by BAR Publishing, 2016.

Printed in England

BAR titles are available from:

	BAR Publishing
	122 Banbury Rd, Oxford, OX2 7BP, UK
EMAIL	info@barpublishing.com
PHONE	+44 (0)1865 310431
FAX	+44 (0)1865 316916
	www.barpublishing.com

Egyptian Tomb Architecture

The Archaeological Facts of Pharaonic Circular Symbolism

In memory of my father; Overseer of Works

Contents

Contents iii
List of figures iv
Preface vii
Acknowledgments x
Map of Egypt with sites discussed in the text highlighted xii
Timeline of events mentioned in the text xiii

Introduction 1
1. Fundamentals of Ancient Egyptian mathematics and architecture 3
2. The Evidence and facts of Egyptian circular proportions 18
    2.1. Example 1: Saqqara - around 2750 B.C. 19
    2.2. Example 2: Meidum – around 2600 B.C. 22
    2.3. Example 3: The Great Pyramid – built around 2550 B.C. 24
    2.4. Example 4: Khufu's King's Chamber walls: around 2550 B.C. ... 29
    2.5. Example 5: Giza site plan – around 2500 B.C. 31
    2.6. Example 6 - Funerary chamber of Amasis II: c.a. 550 B.C. 34
3. The symbolism 36
4. Methodology, analysis and discussion of mathematics 45
5. Arguments from authorities 49
6. Archaeology and philology; fieldwork and deskwork 52
7. Conclusions 61
8. Appendix 1: Secondary Issues 64
9. Appendix 2: Social Context of early Egyptology 66
10. Appendix 3: Egyptian and Greek Mathematics 73
11. Appendix 4: Quotes from the Greeks 82
12. References 83

List of figures

Figure 1 Ma'at, the goddess of truth, providing life in the form of the ankh.. vi
Figure 2 Map of Egypt.. xii
Figure 3 Timeline of events discussed in text... xiii
Figure 4 An Egyptian scribe and the sign representing the tools of the trade... 3
Figure 5 Cubit in hieroglyphs 'cubit' forearm & 'Pharaonic' 4
Figure 6 Tomb of Menna at Thebes - Measuring the harvest 4
Figure 7 The Turin cubit of Amenemope based on Lepsius 5
Figure 8 Turin cubit of Amenemope text 1 6
Figure 9 Turin cubit of Amenemope text 2 7
Figure 10 Diagram of cubit rod showing usual divisions and fractions... 9
Figure 11 Close up of the scale of an 18th dynasty cubit rod of Maya... 10
Figure 12 A Middle Kingdom model of a typical Egyptian Granary 11
Figure 13 Reconstruction of sculptural workshop. NMS, Edinburgh.. 12
Figure 14 Reconstruction of the lost sarcophagus of Menkaure.. 13
Figure 15 Sneferu's Horus name in a Palace 'Serekh' symbol... 14
Figure 16 The Louvre Scribe from the Vth Dynasty 15
Figure 17 Basis for the 7-palm cubit: diagonals and circles made easy.. 16
Figure 18 Symbol of the sun god Re from digit 1 of the royal cubit 17
Figure 19 Saqqara Step Pyramid complex with its temenos perimeter... 19
Figure 20 The Step pyramid of Saqqara – the first pyramid 21
Figure 21 The Collapsed Pyramid at Meidum and fields of the Nile 22
Figure 22 Meidum pyramid with primary dimensions.. 22
Figure 23 The Great Pyramid of Giza: Wonder of the world for 45 centuries 24
Figure 24 Khufu's pyramid with its primary dimensions 25
Figure 25 Seked gradient system - slope of Khufu's Pyramid... 26
Figure 26 Well-preserved casing stones along north face of Khufu 26
Figure 27 3D reconstruction : - Great pyramid core and casing 27
Figure 28 Great Pyramid with interior passages, courses and casing 28
Figure 29 King's Chamber with its primary dimensions... 29
Figure 30 King's Chamber and sarcophagus looking west.. 30
Figure 31 Giza ground plan with primary dimensions 31
Figure 32 Giza plan with primary dimensions... 31
Figure 33 Comparison of approximations 32
Figure 34 Author's 3D representation of Giza topography 32
Figure 35 Reconstruction of Amasis's sepulchral chamber... 34
Figure 36 Tabulated comparison of seven case studies (Factor: 3 significant figures)............................... 35
Figure 37 Symbol for the sun god Re... 36
Figure 38 Shen ring 36
Figure 39 Pectoral necklace of Sit-Hathor-Iunet from c.a. 1870 B.C. 37
Figure 40 Tomb end wall shen ring from TT1 at Deir el-Medina 37
Figure 41 Cartouches from Abydos Kings list :- Sneferu through Menkaure 37
Figure 42 Sneferu's Horus name Neb Ma'at from a royal funerary canopy.. 38
Figure 43 God Heh from Entrance to Ramesses II's jubilee temple.. 38
Figure 44 Horus holding Shen 39
Figure 45 Cartouche shaped sarcophagus of Merneptah from KV8 40
Figure 46 The symbolic tomb of Osiris from the 5th hour of the Amduat in KV34................................... 40
Figure 47 Isis from the sarcophagus of Queen Hatshepsut, recut for Tuthmosis I 41
Figure 48 Lady Shepenhor with the shen rings protecting head... 41
Figure 49 Cartonnage of Djed-Khonsou-iou-ef-ankh 42
Figure 50 Last of the great pyramid builders... 43
Figure 51 Cartouche of pharaoh Khufu from the Great Pyramid 44
Figure 52 Comparison of data from Khufu and Meidum pyramids.. 47
Figure 53 what the developing calculation could have looked like in hieratic 47
Figure 54 Neugerbauer and Petrie – Top philologist and top archaeologist... 52
Figure 55 Hieroglyphics for 'seked', signifying slope angle system... 55

Figure 56 Egyptian construction levelling frames: Cairo Museum 56
Figure 57 RMP Problem 56 – pyramid diagram.. 56
Figure 58 Bent Pyramid with pyramidion found near Red Pyramid superimposed................................ 57
Figure 59 Martin Bernal: Author of 'Black Athena' 59
Figure 60 Khafre's Pyramid with the Great Pyramid behind 64
Figure 61 Ancient design in a modern setting: pyramid of the Louvre 65
Figure 62 Basic Egyptian base-ten hieroglyphic numbering system 73
Figure 63 Stele of Nefertiabet daughter of Khufu 73
Figure 64 Basic Egyptian Hieratic number system 74
Figure 65 Proto Aeolic motif from Naukratis, McLean Museum, Greenock 74
Figure 66 Greek Acrophonic or Herodianic number system 75
Figure 67 Number 539 in alphabetic numbers.. 75
Figure 68 Greek Alphabetic number system with Phoenician symbols below 75
Figure 69 Hieroglyphic sign for hekat grain measure (about 5 litres) 76
Figure 70 Horus Eye Fractions: Individual parts and example 76
Figure 71 Basic Egyptian Hieratic unit fraction system 76
Figure 72 Typical Hieratic unit fraction break down 77
Figure 73 Greek alphabetic number 3+1/4+1/12 77
Figure 74 The antique 6-part 532mm cubit from the Petrie Museum in London 79
Figure 75 Cartouche of Alexander the Great from temple wall in Thebes 80
Figure 76 Replicas of early cartridges with lead balls and a 'cartoccio' food packet.......................... 80
Figure 77 Transcribed glyphs spelling 'Sah Ra' (son of Ra) and ALKSYNDRS 80

Figure 1 Ma'at, the goddess of truth, providing life in the form of the ankh

Preface and acknowledgements

Preface

I give to thee constant harvests, to feed the Two Lands at all times; the sheaves thereof are like the sand of the shore, their granaries approach heaven and their grain heaps are like the mountains.

J. H. Breasted, Ancient Records of Egypt

The objective of this monograph is to describe and explain the meanings underlying some otherwise anomalous archaeological data drawn from the study of Ancient Egypt. An explanation for the phenomena observed has hitherto proved elusive. The data is principally concerned with royal funerary architecture from the Old Kingdom, and the underlying systems of measurement and geometry that were employed therein. As well as providing a description and explanation for the data, this work also has the objective of providing the first synthesis of related cultural information drawn from several different textual and archaeological resources.

The general subject matter is pharaonic funerary architecture from Old Kingdom Egypt, and this work focuses specifically on the circular proportions deliberately incorporated into the tomb designs by the architects. This symbolism served to define a protective perimeter surrounding the deceased pharaoh's tomb. The Ancient Egyptians believed in the active power of this tradition, and considered that it provided eternal protection for the pharaoh's resting place, thus allowing his spirit to ascend to the heavenly paradise where his ancestors awaited.

Much of the raw data supporting this interpretation has been in the public domain for decades, and so this work is in part an attempt to reform mainstream understanding of some well-known facts regarding Egyptian tomb architecture.

The length of this thesis means that I have not been able to publish it for peer review in any academic journal before releasing it to the public in this monograph. The intention is, however, that this first edition be used to allow peer review to take place, with an eye to including constructive comments and feedback into a second edition that will be lengthier. Peer review is a vital part of the research process, and so this first edition should be considered to be an interim report of an on-going peer-reviewed study.

While most of the data is already well known to those familiar with the subject, some of it is completely new. The most substantial difference between this work and past works, however, is the synthesis of all the data and references into one volume, into one historical narrative, and the proper analysis of the meanings of the symbolism within its cultural context.

This work is addressed to both Egyptologists and historians of science and mathematics alike. As such, I have had to include general background from both subject areas that specialists in the respective subjects may feel is superfluous, or covering overly familiar ground yet again. Nevertheless, it is necessary to present background to both fields in this way precisely because the synthesis must straddle both academic subject areas, and must therefore allow the information from one area to be accessible to specialists from the other.

This approach also has the advantage of allowing informed amateurs from both subject areas to access the information and meanings arising from the data.

The assimilation, synthesis, analysis and interpretation of all the existing archaeological, architectural and textual evidence relating to this subject matter has never been attempted or completed before now.

The extensive use of 3-dimensional reconstructions to analyse the data and symbolism is also partly new.

Continuing debate regarding these data, facts and conclusions is always welcome, however, in my opinion it is high time that the wider academic community of Egyptologists clearly accepts the basic facts and conclusions that are outlined in this report. The failure to accept the basic conclusions regarding the facts of the matter has left a level of uncertainly hovering over the subject, and this uncertainty has certainly contributed to the proliferation of alternative theories that have attempted to explain the anomalous evidence, many of them highly speculative and some of them even verging on the fantastic. It is hoped that this new synthesis of the data in an academic but hopefully digestible format will encourage the acceptance of the basic facts, and provide impetus to a new movement to examine the cultural meanings in more detail.

As well as discussing the achievements of the ancient Egyptians, this work responds to some of the conclusions drawn by 19th and early 20th century desk-based scholars called 'philologists', who followed primarily text led lines of enquiry, and who often neglected aspects of the field archaeology of Egypt. As such, it is the culmination of an on-going and vigorous discussion regarding the evidence of the abilities of the ancient Egyptian scribes, surveyors and architects that I have been involved with for at least eight years now. It is now time for archaeologists and Egyptologists to reclaim the academic field of Egypt from the non-specialists, and specialists from other areas, who have often re-interpreted the archaeological data from Egypt to match their own particular agendas and theories.

Given the convoluted history of the subject, and the ideological forces that have always surrounded the study

Preface and acknowledgements

of Ancient Egypt, it is doubtful that this will be the last word. Nevertheless, by organising and synthesising the facts and data in a way that makes them more accessible to current and future scholars, it should be possible for due credit to be given, and continue to be given, to the Egyptians for their awesome monumental, technical and artistic achievements.

It may seem that this subject matter and the related archaeological facts are overly arcane, or unrelated to the modern world, but in fact this is far from the case. Many of the issues relating to Ancient Egypt have shaped the modern world at a fundamental level, and continue to influence 21st century society in a myriad of ways. Some of the most important social issues are discussed in chapter 9 of this report. The study of ancient history can help us understand the modern world, and vice versa, and so the relevance of this synthesis should be carefully evaluated.

Many scholars have used research and study as a means to tackle social issues, and archaeology is particularly effective in this respect: "The history of archaeology is nothing if not the record of a continual struggle by scholars to rise above the biases, preconceptions, and delusions of previous generations....It is also....a distinctive mode of behaviour, in which the participants cannot help but be deeply affected by the hopes, fears, and power relationships of their own societies" (Silberman 1998: 268).

There are many problems in our societies that are legacies of very old ideologies, and the most effective way to tackle modern problems is often to study them, understand them, and finally rectify the problems with the ideologies from the past that created them. Ideology can and does alter how we think about the world around us, and this is often imposed on us through biased interpretations and misrepresentations of past events, mostly in the popular media. This means that false interpretations of historical events can have serious consequences and influences in the present.

As a generally optimistic person, I believe that people try to do 'the right thing' at any moment, and act on the best information they have available at any one time. It is therefore imperative that people have balanced, broadly truthful and accurate accounts of the present and the past to work from, otherwise they will be making decisions based on flawed premises.

One of the many historical subjects of study that have been affected by racism and religious ideologies is Ancient Egypt. When dealing with very ancient monuments such as those of pharaonic Egypt, any historical interpretations distorted by ideology can be very old indeed, and so the effects of these misrepresentations can be quite profound. The culture of Egypt has influenced almost all subsequent European, Asian and African civilisations, but a quite astonishing quantity of different interrelated ideologies has also been projected back onto the ancient society through the centuries. At times its seems that unravelling all the flawed ideologies associated with these ancient monuments is a task almost as daunting as building them must have been.

One of the most dominating symbolisms seen throughout Ancient Egypt, and which is touched on in this book, was the iconography relating to the 'unification of the two lands'. The two lands of Egypt were the wide delta region leading north down to the Mediterranean Sea, and the long thin Nile valley leading South, up into the mountains and deserts of Africa. The iconography relating to the unification of these areas is seen all over the monuments and artwork of Egypt, up and down the Nile valley. Composite crowns of Upper Egypt and Lower Egypt were worn by the pharaoh, the 'Lord of the Two Lands', sitting on thrones dedicated to Upper and Lower Egypt. Ancient Egypt's rulers were devoted to keeping their people together and united, and to avoiding division and social conflict in their world. They attempted to bring everyone together under common emblems, but they also worked to incorporate each people's unique identity into the country as a whole. Each town or region had its own gods and symbols, and they were also an integral part of the larger pharaonic state. There are many parallels between ancient Egypt and modern organisations of international government, and we can surely learn some lessons about stability and peace from a civilisation that endured for so many centuries.

As the Egyptians seem to have understood, all individuals, and individual groups, from cities to families, have their own identities and traditions that must be respected. While a return to traditional dogmatic religion or superstitions that dominate society is not desirable in a democracy, people's right to follow any tradition of their choice should be respected in the modern world, and incorporated into the larger system. As long as it does not impact excessively negatively on others, and works within the laws of the land, everyone should have the right to follow, or adopt, or deviate from whatever code of conduct they consider to be their own.

This respect for differences, and the importance of reflecting this through cultural symbols, is really the 'take home' message of this introduction, and is a message for the modern world taken from the civilisation of Ancient Egypt. It is just this sort of lesson, with a social relevance for the present day, which makes the study of Ancient Egypt, and ancient history as a whole, so worthwhile.

This issue was, nevertheless, just one of the important traditional concerns of the people of the Nile valley that was addressed within their complex and elaborate artistic system.

Several such important iconographic concepts are discussed in this work, but it is mainly devoted to one symbol in particular, the circle, which was deliberately incorporated into royal funerary architecture. This was included to ensure the stability, longevity and eternal

Preface and acknowledgements

protection of the pharaoh, and the Egyptian universe he ruled. The ways in which this symbolism was incorporated into the architecture, and the precise iconography that was being represented, are explained and illustrated below.

It is important to appreciate that the Ancient Egyptian people genuinely believed in the active power of this symbolism. Indeed, it was precisely this active belief in the power of symbols that made them so effective in influencing daily life in the Nile valley.

Finally, we should of course thank the Ancient Egyptians themselves for all their hard work. The next few chapters are concerned with giving them full credit, where it's due, for their magnificent and enduring monuments.

I hope you will enjoy experiencing the architectural magic of Ancient Egypt as much as I always have.

The author can be contacted through the email address arky@hotmail.co.uk.

A website dedicated to the ongoing research can be found at www.Arky.eu/

Preface and acknowledgements

Acknowledgments

In acknowledging individuals who have helped me complete this work, I would first like to recognise the late Professor Sir William Matthew Flinders Petrie (1853-1942) for dedicating his life to uncovering the facts about Ancient Egypt, and revealing the everyday lives of the people who lived along the Nile valley. His fascinating works have often provided me with good guidance over the years, and his exemplary attention to detail has reminded me to be dedicated to the facts at all times. 'Observation of trifles' and a passion for detail was his methodology, or as the archaeologist Sir Mortimer Wheeler described: "By his incredible ingenuity complex problems were liable to be rendered excessively simple and surmountable, simple problems might be tangled into inextricable complexities" (Wheeler 1953: 91). For those not familiar with Petrie, he became the first Professor of Egyptology in the England, after his long-time supporter, writer and amateur Egyptologist Amelia Edwards (1831-1892), left a substantial sum for the foundation of the first department of Egyptology at University College, London, in her will. Amelia Edwards had understood how brilliant Petrie was since he published the results of the theodolite survey of the Giza plateau, which he carried out single handed in 1882, and she supported him throughout his prolific career. Petrie went on to dominate excavation in Egypt, and worked in the region for fully 70 years. This work draws heavily on Petrie's many surveys, excavation reports and books.

Secondly I would like to thank all of those who have helped me familiarise myself with the facts of this matter, and provided me with the references and guidance to study the subject in more depth. This includes those who have disagreed with me and explained where I was going wrong (which happened frequently). Only by being able to swallow my pride and accept that my position was often untenable was I finally able to move towards a more tenable position. Over time I came to understand that this is in fact a fundamental element of good research methodology, and a good approach to life in general. I also thank those who have dogmatically disagreed with me, despite the presentation of supporting evidence, as this has made me ever more determined to find and demonstrate the truth of the matter. All of these colleagues have my sincere thanks for engaging in several years of interesting debate over this subject, and I look forwards to continuing this discussion with them.

I would next like to pay tribute to Graham Oaten of Melbourne, Australia who very sadly died in this summer of this year. It is thanks to his hard work, in cooperation with his colleague Ronald Birdsall, that an online version of Flinders Petrie's 1882/3 survey of Giza, *The Pyramids and Temples of Gizeh,* was first scanned from an original edition, converted into an early form of HTML code, and made available to the general public.

In 2003, Graham and Ronald entered into a collaboration to detect, edit and correct several errors and legibility problems associated with Petrie's handwritten record of the Great Pyramid course elevations. This fully corrected survey data is available via their website at www.ronaldbirdsall.com/gizeh/. The report is still the most comprehensive source of information regarding the basic dimensions of the Giza monuments (Petrie 1883).

Jon Bodsworth has my additional thanks for allowing me to use his beautiful photographs again, without restriction, and his high precision digital reconstructions of the architecture of Giza and the sarcophagus of Menkaure. He is a fine example of the type of generous gentleman scholar that seems to have been so familiar in Egypt during the 19th century. I would like to thank Ken Bakeman for his graphical representation of the Turin cubit, and Dr Angela McDonald for her superb transcription, translation and graphical presentation of the hieroglyphic text from the decorated ancient cubit rule, which is included here for the first time ever.

Next, I would like to thank all my friends, family and loved ones who have put up with so much from me during the years that I have been chasing this wild goose of a subject. I hope one day they may come to understand why I was prepared to spend so much of my time, money and effort on this subject matter, and to use up so much of their goodwill in the process. The truth is that this is an important historical matter that stretches across many centuries, and deeply influences many fields of knowledge. In particular, clear evidence of some racist biases and falsehoods that had crept into the scholarship surrounding the subject had to be tackled directly, at all times, relentlessly and vigorously.

We are all the products of our families, friends, work colleagues and teachers, so in many ways, my family, friends and colleagues are all partly responsible for this book. The academic, engineering, mathematical, social and rationalist traditions of Scottish and European society have given me a firm foundation to work from, access to the tools of rational enquiry, and the ability to speculate, but speculate sceptically.

For all this, I am grateful, and I hope that this publication can go some way towards paying back the debt that I owe to my community

Finally, I would also like to thank those who have taught me the more serious academic, practical and theoretical methods of archaeological research, at the University of Glasgow, and out in the field, and in particular all of my fellow archaeologists based in Glasgow. The motto of the University of Glasgow is *Via Veritas Vita*, the way, the truth, the life, and it is an adage that has inspired me in my research. The words echo the ancient Egyptians' dedication to truth, personified by the goddess Ma'at, with her feather headdress representing the delicate weighing of the balances of the scales of truth. The

Preface and acknowledgements

ancient Egyptian scribes also represented the importance of life through the symbol of the ankh. I therefore decided to begin this monograph with a figure of the goddess Ma'at providing life through the ankh [Figure 1]. This is intended to serve as a reminder of the importance of these eternal and vital concepts to daily life in the present, and also to the scholarly recording of daily life from the past.

Preface and acknowledgements

Map of Egypt with sites discussed in the text highlighted

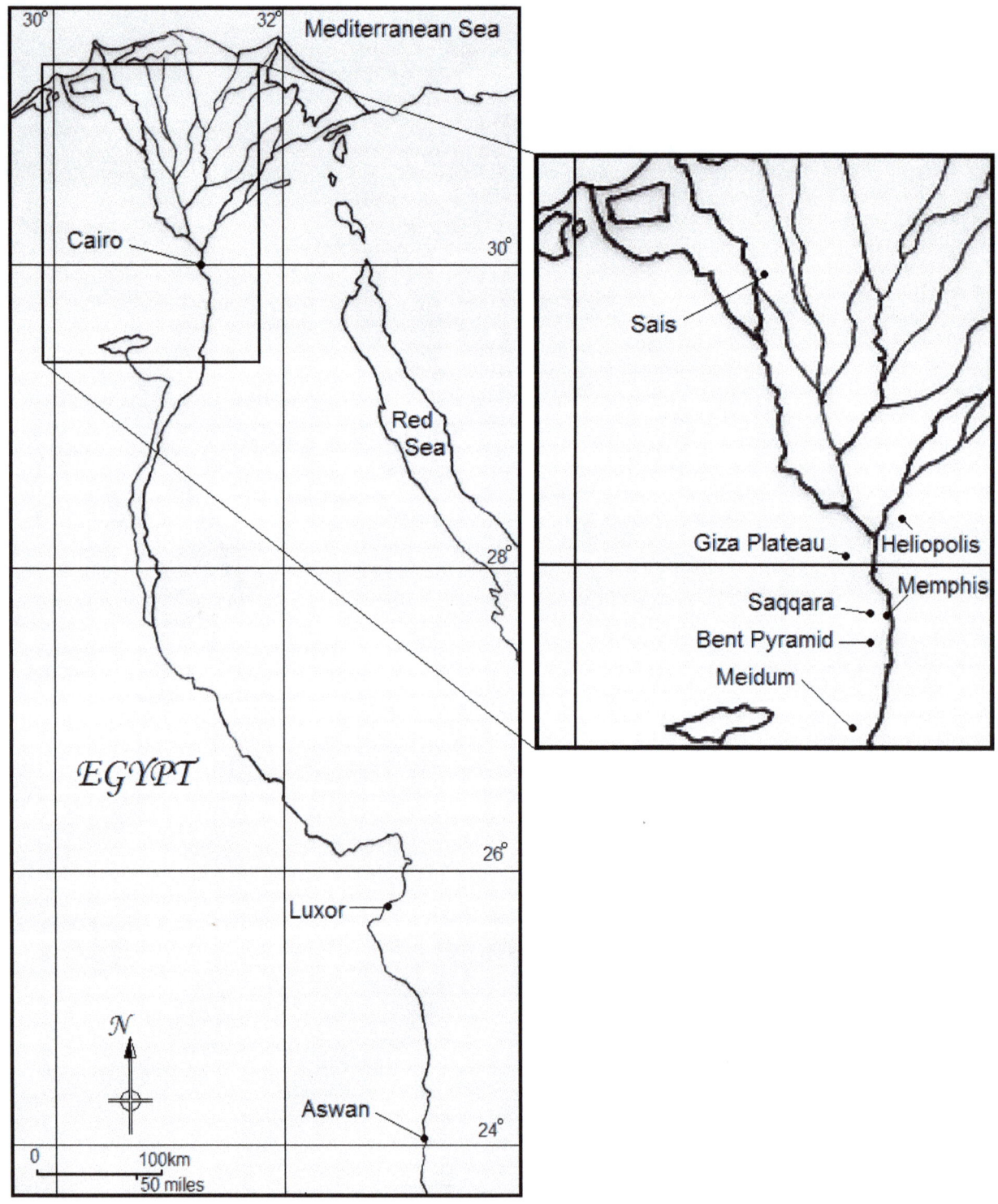

Figure 2 Map of Egypt

Preface and acknowledgements

Timeline of events mentioned in the text

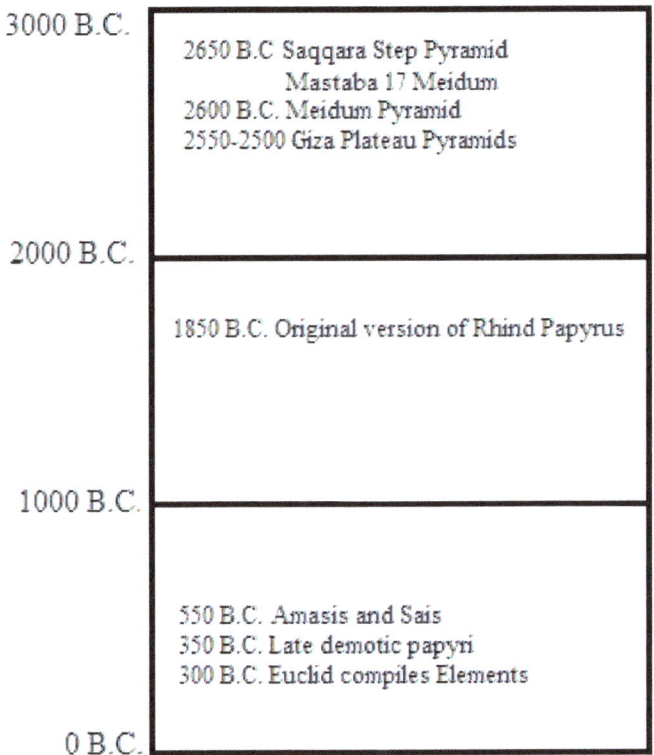

Predynastic Egypt:	Prior to 3,100 B.C.
Protodynastic Egypt:	3200 – 3000 B.C.
Early Dynastic Egypt:	3000 – 2686 B.C.
Old Kingdom:	**2686 – 2134 B.C.**
First Intermediate Period:	2134 – 2030 B.C.
Middle Kingdom:	**2030 – 1640 B.C.**
Second Intermediate Period:	1640 – 1570 B.C.
New Kingdom:	**1570 – 1070 B.C.**
Third Intermediate Period:	1070 – 664 B.C.
Late Period:	**663 – 332 B.C.**
Ptolemaic Period:	332 – 30 B.C.

Figure 3 Timeline of events discussed in text

Introduction

"Without Petrie there would have been no archaeology, we should still have been bound by the written word and the dry-as-dust philologists and antiquarians"
(Murray 1963: 317).

This work re-iterates, summarises and supplements some orthodox facts regarding Old Kingdom (c.a. 2686 BC – 2134 BC) royal tomb architecture that were uncovered by top Egyptologists during the late 19th and 20th centuries. The basic facts, obtained directly from the archaeology, demonstrate the use of circular proportions in funerary architecture for traditional symbolic reasons. As well as reiterating the facts of this matter, this work supplements them with up to date and new information, and provides a synthesis and interpretation of all the data, textual as well as archaeological, into one historical reconstruction.

Despite the formidable reputations and vast experience of the expert Egyptologists who first uncovered these facts, some of their conclusions were subsequently obscured from mainstream Egyptology. This was firstly due to incorrect and unfounded counter conclusions reached by non-specialists from outside the archaeological field, and secondly, due to a degree of ingrained academic cultural racism and bias regarding Egypt, and the facts that had been uncovered there.

The developments made during the Old Kingdom were undoubtedly formidable, but the work by 19th and 20th century Egyptologists to recover the facts about the period was no less impressive. Due to the ideological force associated with the recovery of ancient history, for religious, nationalist and political reasons, many top people became involved with research into Egypt, and very high standards of scholarship and publication were attained. From the monumental work by Napoleon's 'savants', *Description de l'Egypte*, through Flinders Petrie's brilliant survey of Giza, or Maspero and Sayce's heavyweight *Dawn of Civilisation*, and on to the modern publications by Kemp, Lehner or Weeks and their colleagues, Egypt has often if not always been home to the highest standards of applied scholarship and technical publishing skill. Perhaps it is no coincidence that Egypt was the homeland of the first scribes to put pen to 'paper'.

Unfortunately Egypt has also attracted more than its fair share of cranks, mystagogues and 'pyramidiots', ready to project their own mystical or ethnocentric beliefs onto an ancient culture where it does not belong. The nineteenth century in particular was a time of fertile imaginations, and Egypt, as one of the central ideological fields of study, attracted much speculative and fantastic attention.

Even today, many of these speculative ideas have an enduring and considerable influence on the study of Ancient Egypt, and it is only by understanding the background to all of these ideas, and their origins, that it is possible to correctly eliminate their enduring influences entirely from the historical facts.

After this introduction, the first chapter of the book outlines what is known about the basic Egyptian technical systems, such as the written numbers, the cubit measurement rules and simple seked angle measurement methods, and why they developed within the Old Kingdom cultural context. These are the systems that we need to understand and use to interpret the Ancient Egyptian architecture.

The second chapter then details six separate cases where the traditional symbolism of the circle was incorporated into the pharaonic funerary architecture using these traditional methods - see [Figure 2] for locations of the sites in the text.

The third chapter then explores what this circular symbolism meant, and why it was incorporated into and around pharaonic funerary architecture. The chapter effectively concludes the presentation of the evidence central to this thesis.

The fourth chapter then reviews the methodology employed to carry out this study, and further logical conclusions that can be drawn out from the facts. It concludes with the construction of a probable developmental sequence through which the geometric skills observable in the architectural evidence were developed during the third and fourth dynasties.

The fifth chapter then reviews the written opinions of experts who have already, quite correctly, confirmed the use of this symbolism in the royal architecture.

The sixth chapter then discusses the academic studies that did not arrive at the correct conclusions (and there are many) regarding this matter, and identifies the various reasons that they failed to do so. It focuses on the politics of more recent times, the struggle between archaeologists in the field and armchair textual philologists over the distant past, and over the interpretation of the data and facts about the past. The conclusion of this analysis include the realisation that academic cultural racism, with its roots in 19th century European geopolitical strategies, still distorts the way some modern Western scholars see the distant past.

It is the intention of this work to rectify that situation as far as is possible.

The conclusions chapter then summarises the findings and discussed the results, while four appendices then review related issues from Egyptian and Greek scholarship that are of secondary importance, but of general interest and relevance to the main thesis.

At the higher level, the book attempts to synthesise the diverse textual and archaeological data that already exists into one historical reconstruction, and as such it fills an

Introduction

academic gap between several existing publications. These publications are Petrie's *Wisdom of the Egyptians (1940)*, Gillings's *Mathematics in the time of the Pharaohs (1982)*, Edwards's *The Pyramids of Egypt (1979)*, Wilkinson's *Symbol and Magic in Egyptian Art (1999)* and Arnold's *Building in Egypt: Pharaonic Stone Masonry (1991)*. All of these excellent books are clearly written and easily read, and any readers unfamiliar with the details of Egyptian Old Kingdom architecture would do well to concentrate on these in the first instance for solid background information. None of the books give a complete description of the Egyptians' use of circular symbolism in funerary architecture, but all provide valuable pieces of the jigsaw that leads to an accurate reconstruction of the Ancient Egyptians' intended designs.

Lastly, much of the data and many of the references and quotes included in this study have been assembled together over many years, and whilst every effort has been made to ensure consistency and accuracy throughout, I can offer no guarantees. The reader is forewarned to check all references for his or herself, as correct methodology demands, but at the same time, none of the conclusions herein rely on any single detail, and all are in many respects interdependent. While 'god is in the detail', the cross checking of the various facts, and the integrity of the whole raft of supporting evidence mean that at some point the researcher must accept the bigger picture of the past that has been developed by the archaeologists and surveyors, with confidence, rather than become more and more lost in the uncertainty of minutiae and details. That is a fate that has befallen too many armchair philologists in the past, and the archaeologist must avoid this pitfall.

As a friend of mine once succinctly summarised for me, "*it is the whole picture that is the point*". Nevertheless, the only way to truly understand the big picture in all its detail is to get out there and visit the archaeological sites, and see the real ancient artefacts. While it may not be necessary to learn to walk like an Egyptian, it is certainly necessary to learn to think like the scribes, surveyors, architects and builders of the ancient civilisation that evolved on the banks of the mighty Nile.

Chapter 1.   Fundamentals of Old Egyptian mathematics and architecture

1. Fundamentals of Ancient Egyptian mathematics and architecture

"Sesostris also, they declared, made a division of the soil of Egypt among the inhabitants, assigning square plots of ground of equal size to all, and obtaining his chief revenue from the rent which the holders were required to pay him year by year. If the river carried away any portion of a man's plot, he appeared before the king and related what had happened; upon which the king sent persons to examine, and determine by measurement the exact extent of the loss; and thenceforth only such a rent was demanded of him as was proportionate to the reduced size of his land. From this practice, I think, geometry first came to be known in Egypt, whence it passed to Greece." (Histories II: 109) (Herodotus. 1996: 159).

This chapter outlines what we know about the basic Egyptian technical systems that were applied to the tomb architecture, and how they first developed. In it I discuss a gradual increase in complexity that took place during the Old Kingdom, from basic written numbers, through to the cubit measurement system, and eventually on to true geometry. Only by fully understanding the historical development of the Old Kingdom and its practical technologies can the archaeology and architectural symbolism produced by that culture be correctly interpreted. This is the approach that this work will take throughout in presenting the facts of the subject within their cultural contexts. Eventually, we must learn to think like an Egyptian.

Famously, as the Greek historian and traveller Herodotus commented, Egypt was 'The Gift of the Nile'. This is certainly a truism, which is why it is so widely quoted, but the Egyptian people themselves had much to do to manage the fertile fields on the banks of the Nile, and to organise the irrigation, sowing and harvesting of the crops that grew there so rapidly. The combination of an abundant water supply and fertile soils in a warm climate, with almost continual hot sunshine, was ideal for agriculture, and the Egyptians made full and efficient use of their natural resources.

To understand the Egyptian pharaonic civilisation it is essential to appreciate that it was built on industrial scale grain production. This is the cultural context of the Old Kingdom, and every facet of their lifestyle and the developments they made were grounded in the reality of the fields and the grain that they grew there. It was once a Christian tradition that the pyramids were the "granaries of Joseph", and this is an apt analogy. The population, the civilisation, and the great monuments of Egypt were ultimately built on the energy and nutrition supplied by the fields of grain, and to understand the developments that this civilisation made in mathematics, geometry, art and architecture, we need to understand how these inventions were born out of agricultural necessity (Brock 2005).

Crop production flourished increasingly from at least 3500 B.C. until it was carried out on an industrial scale during the Old Kingdom. To coordinate and encourage this growth, symbolic technical systems such as writing and numeracy had to be developed that allowed the rulers to allocate, measure, record and fairly distribute land, quantities of grain, numbers of animals and different types of produce. Numeracy, for example, allowed individual resource 'units' to be quantified, such as numbers of fields or at the bi-annual cattle counts that became an important event in the Egyptian calendar. Knowing and recording just how many cattle one possessed, for example, was not just a matter of status but was potentially a matter of life and death in the case of crop failure or plague. Knowing and recording how much fallow land one possessed on which to graze them was no less important.

To solve the problems associated with industrial scale agriculture, the Egyptians developed some ingenious systems that we still use today. They first developed the base-ten numbering system, and the system of writing onto papyrus with ink. Writing was a complex and efficient method for recording large volumes of data in a small and portable 'paper' format, but it required a skilled core of people who were trained in the practical and abstract techniques for communicating symbolically (i.e. writing). These people were the scribes. The diagram below shows an Egyptian scribe alongside the hieroglyph representing the tools of their trade. These tools were a jar for mixing water, black and red pigment palettes, and a brush holder, all attached to a portable carrier that was worn over the shoulder [Figure 4].

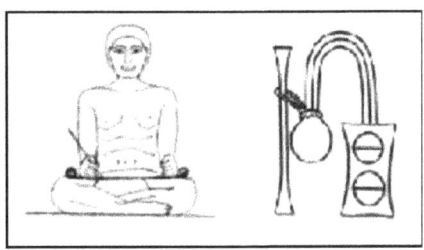

Figure 4 An Egyptian scribe and the sign representing the tools of the trade

Egyptian writing, today called hieroglyphic writing, was developed as early as 3,500 B.C. and was in widespread use by the Old Kingdom alongside base ten numerical symbols [See appendix 3]. Efficient agriculture nevertheless required much more than simple counting and recording, and new and more complex systems were devised by necessity.

The first of the new skills devised that is of importance here was the ability to measure lengths, and not only that, but the ability to measure lengths in a way that different people could refer to and understand.

Chapter 1. Fundamentals of Old Egyptian mathematics and architecture

This important technical concept underpinned many of the subsequent developments and effectively formed the world's first standardised weights and measurement system. In Egypt we know that linear measurement was based on the royal or pharaonic cubit. The royal cubit standard was in place as early as the 3rd dynasty, and probably somewhat before this. This measurement system allowed agricultural produce and agricultural land to be measured against a fixed benchmark. Most importantly for the bureaucrats, it allowed taxation to be applied to surplus produce in a regulated fashion.

Figure 5 Cubit in hieroglyphs 'cubit' forearm & 'Pharaonic'

The tomb mural below provided a great deal of information regarding the way in which the measurement systems were used to tax agricultural land [Figure 6]. As part of this daily story of agricultural life, one of the fundamental systems used was the knotted cords that served to measure the fields. The pharaonic cubit measurement standard was employed to ensure that this was done accurately and fairly. The ropes were often of 100 cubits, or 1 'khet', or just over 52m. This sort of measuring underpinned the development of their mathematics, geometry and architecture, and so all of these were intimately related to the development of the Egyptian's agricultural economy as a whole.

Once the cubit had been used to measure the lengths and widths of the relevant fields, a calculation had to be performed to quantify the total 'size' of each field, which is effectively its area. As the Greek historian Herodotus understood, and confirmed in the quote at the head of this chapter, this sort of calculation signalled the birth of Geometry; which is Greek for 'earth measuring'.

"From this practice, I think, geometry first came to be known in Egypt, whence it passed to Greece".

As well as enabling standardised measuring of lengths and areas of fields, the cubit system was also used to quantify and redistribute grain by volume. These sorts of increasingly complex agricultural calculations, involving lengths, areas and then volumes, formed the impetus and the basis for the development of mathematics and geometry. Within the earliest developmental phases of state formation and economic growth, measurement and mathematics came to play a central role for solving the practical daily challenges of agricultural subsistence and the management of surpluses on a large scale. On the Rhind Mathematical Papyrus, which will be discussed in detail later, we can see that examples pertaining to the calculation, division and distribution of volumes of agricultural produce predominate (Chace 1929; Gillings 1982: 120; Imhausen 2003).

To be really organised and efficient, produce such as wheat, barley or papyrus had to be measured by volume or weighed in bulk, on a fixed and comparable basis, and quantified in a way that everyone could understand. To do this, special scribes dedicated to measuring the land and managing the surpluses in the granaries were trained and employed.

Figure 6 Tomb of Menna at Thebes - Measuring the harvest

The hieroglyphic text below, transcribed, translated and published here for the first time [Figure 8] is from the decorated cubit of Amenemope, a nobleman known as the 'overseer of the double granary of the lord of the two lands'. The cubit is now in the Turin museum and is specimen number 3; museum catalogue number 6347. Amenemope's wooden cubit rod was found at Saqqara or nearby Memphis, dates to the end of the 18th Dynasty, c.a. 1300 B.C., and is inscribed with the 'dedication' or hieroglyphic prayer text displayed below.

Chapter 1. Fundamentals of Old Egyptian mathematics and architecture

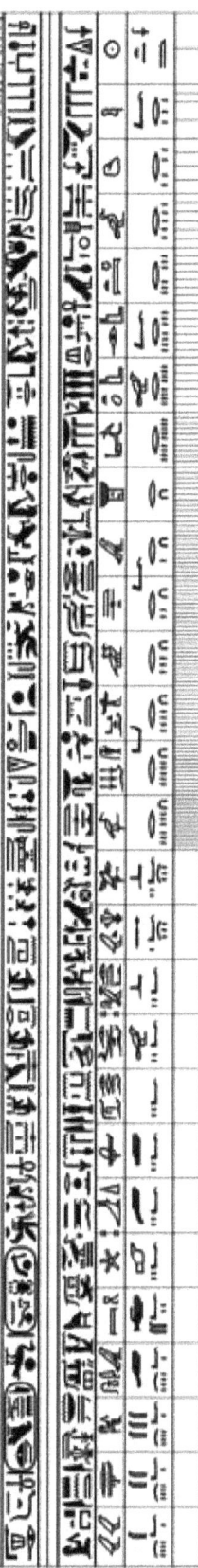

Figure 7 The Turin cubit of Amenemope based on Lepsius

Chapter 1. Fundamentals of Old Egyptian mathematics and architecture

ḥtp di nsw nṯrw nbw mḥ-nsw di=sn ʿḥʿw nfr m ʿnḫ tp t3

An offering that the king gives to all the gods of the royal cubit so that they may give a perfect span of life upon earth,

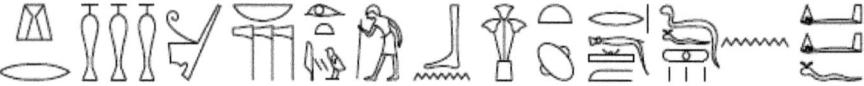

ḫr ḥswt n nb nṯrw irt i3w bn ḫ3t r mḥ m ḏf3w n dd=f

possessing the praises of the Lord of the gods, the experiencing of old age without illness,

a mouth filled with provisions of his giving,

sm3 t3 m-ḫft-ḥr nb=s m smyt imntt w3st m wḏ nṯr pn špsy imn ḥry st wrt

a burial in the presence of its lord in the western desert of Thebes, according to the command of this noble god, Amun, Lord of the Great Place,

n k3 n ḥsy n nṯr nfr rḫ-nsw m3ʿ mry=f b3kt-t3wy imy-r-pr n p3 st n rʿ imy-r šnwty n nb t3wy

for the ka of the praised one of the perfect god, the king's true acquaintance, his beloved, the tribute of the Two Lands, the steward of the seat of Re, the overseer of the double granary of the Lord of the Two Lands,

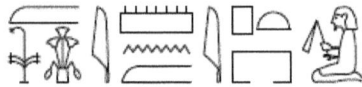

m šmʿ mḥ imn-m-ipt

in the south and the north, Amenemope.

Figure 8 Turin cubit of Amenemope text 1

Chapter 1. Fundamentals of Old Egyptian mathematics and architecture

[ꜥnḫ] nṯr nfr kꜣ nṯrw ḥw ḏfꜣw n ḥnmmt

[Life to!] The perfect god, the ka/food of the gods, the sustenance and provisions of the sun-people,

nsw nṯry mnḫ sḫrw ity nḫt

divine king, effective of plans, victorious sovereign,

rs-tp n rḫyt sḫb kmt

alert for the common people, the one who delights the Black Land

spd-ḥr is tꜣ

keen-sighted, the ? of the land,

tmw ḥr nḥm bn gr snmḥ=sn m ꜥnḫ wꜣs

everyone keeps rejoicing without stopping, they pray for life and power

n nsw bity ḏsr-ḫprw-rꜥ stp-n-rꜥ sꜣ-rꜥ ḥr-m-ḥb mry-imn ꜥnḫ ḏt ir ḥr-ꜥ

for the King of Upper and Lower Egypt, Djeserkheperura Chosen of Ra, Son of Ra, Horemhab Beloved of Amun, living forever, acting with authority (?).

Figure 9 Turin cubit of Amenemope text 2

Chapter 1. Fundamentals of Old Egyptian mathematics and architecture

The remarkable offering prayer speaks of the relationships between the cubit, the gods, the king, the commoners and the 'people of the sun', who may have been the ruling scribal class. Talk of provisions, plenty, the double granary, of being effective of plans and alert for the common people clearly shows that it was the responsibility of the scribal class to ensure the effective management of crop production and surplus, and to ensure the longevity and health of the whole Egyptian society.

At Thebes, several tombs have been discovered decorated with colourful artwork that celebrated the lives of four royal surveyors. The 'harpedonaptae' or the 'rope-stretchers' who measured the fields with regularly knotted lengths of ropes were not individually named. The master surveyors, however, each had a tomb decorated with scenes attesting to their achievements in the service of the pharaonic state. The deceased were described variously as "scribe of the fields of the lord of the two lands of upper and lower Egypt", "scribe of the reckoning of grain", "overseer of the granaries of upper and lower Egypt" (Brock 2005).

Agricultural surveyors were employed to re-measure and allocate field system plots and check them for taxation purposes, while 'accountants' drafted up detailed tables of produce and temple possessions (Kemp 2005: 164 - 169).

The passage below from the 'instructions of Amenemope, dates to the New Kingdom and also attests to the close relationship between the scribes, measures, field, taxes, granaries and the king (Lichtheim 2006: 448).

Made by the overseer of fields, experienced in his office,
The offspring of a scribe of Egypt,
The overseer of grains who controls the measure,
Who sets the harvest-dues for his lord,
Who registers the islands of new land,
In the great name of his majesty,
Who records the markers on the borders of fields,
Who acts for the king in his listing of taxes,
Who makes the land-register of Egypt,
The scribe who determines the offerings for all the gods,
Who gives land-leases to the people,
The overseer of grains, [provider] of food,
Who supplies the granary with grains.

Examples on the Rhind Mathematical Papyrus, the most comprehensive surviving textual source of information regarding Old and Middle Kingdom mathematical capabilities, show methods for distributing produce equally between several men, including grain, cattle and loaves (Gillings 1982: 120), and methods for calculating volumes of cylindrical granaries (Gillings 1982: 146) in units known as 'hekats' of around a litre in volume. Other examples from the Moscow Mathematical papyrus show methods for calculating quantities of beer, loaves and areas of cloth. The two-dimensional and three-dimensional geometric problems included many examples calculated in cubits.

The Egyptian 'pharaonic' or 'royal' cubit standard rule [Figure 5] was, from its earliest appearance, 52.3-52.4cm in length. It was subdivided into 7 palms, each of which was further subdivided into 4 digits, making 28 parts in all. Division of the rules into 7 palms is at first sight remarkably odd, as the most common subdivisions used in normal construction, those representing halves, quarters and thirds of a rule, were not available. The 7 palm rule is therefore apparently quite unsuited to linear measurement. Despite its historical significance, no really in-depth studies of the system have been carried out since those produced by the Egyptologists Lepsius and Petrie in the 19th and early 20th centuries, so that there is no definitive explanation for the choice of 7 palms, or 28 parts in all (Petrie 1926; Arnold 1991: 251; Lepsius 2000). The 7 palm system was unsuited to basic applied linear measurement, but there are other attributes of this setup that make it well suited to the Egyptian unit fraction system, and to plane geometry of the sort that was applied on a daily basis in Egyptian agriculture and construction, and it is to these issues that we will turn for an explanation at the end of this chapter.

As a practical tool, the symbolic evidence suggests that it evolved from earlier, non-standardised measurement systems based on measuring against parts of the body, reminiscent of modern day 'rules of thumb'. This means that it constituted an 'anthropometric' measure. Nevertheless, rather than being based on any real forearm that was used as a benchmark, as the hieroglyph above may suggest to some, the overall length of the measure was most likely based on an arbitrary, roughly approximated, precursor that became the fixed standard through habit and repetition. In fact, at 52.3-52.4cm it is excessively long for any historical forearm, so it is very unlikely it was based on any actual body measurement.

Recent ideas that there was an older 'common cubit' measure that was 6 palms in length instead of the 7 of the 'Royal' measure are not based on any secure evidence (Iverson 1975: 14-16). A couple of shorter rods divided into 6 palms are known from later periods, but these may have had more to do with the 3 x 6 square grids used for wall paintings of figures (Robins 1994: 88), and did not constitute a different measurement system. By way of cross-referenced supporting evidence for the use of the 7 palm cubit, the famous Palermo stone carved towards the end of the fifth dynasty clearly shows annual flood levels recorded back to the Early Dynastic period. For Khufu's reign (the pharaoh for whom the Great Pyramid was built), an inundation level of 3 cubits, 6 palms, 3 1/2 digits is listed, which means that the cubit in use then certainly had more than 6 palms, and this is considered the most secure evidence for the 7 part unit from the Old Kingdom. At times, 6ths and 3rds of cubits are recorded, such as on the Reisner papyrus, and one sixth of the seven palm cubit may have been known colloquially as 'a

Chapter 1. Fundamentals of Old Egyptian mathematics and architecture

sandal' or 'a sandal-width', but again it did not constitute another separate system, but an unusual way to a subdivide the 7 palm measure (M. Verner, *MDAIK* 37 (1981), 479-81). This probably evolved due to the demands of practical construction when division into thirds is often necessary. In summary, there is no evidence that any other standard system apart from the 7 palm, 28 digit cubit was ever used in the Old Kingdom.

Rather than think of the 7 palm royal cubit as being an especially long measure reserved for an elite class, as its name perhaps suggests, it is probably better to think of it simply as the 'official cubit'.

But how do we know what size this 'official cubit' was?

From excavations at the third dynasty Saqqara Step Pyramid complex (c.a. 2650 B.C.), Egyptologists Firth and Quibell noted, based on Lauer's work, that:

"A length, evidently of 2 cubits, marked out by vertical lines in red on a wall of the South Princess' court gave **0m.524** as the cubit of the time, and this length divided into the main dimensions produced a long series of whole numbers with a very small margin of error. The numbers so obtained are most frequently multiples of 10 or 5" (Lauer 1931: 59; Firth, Quibell et al. 1935).

Flinders Petrie similarly derived [in inches] what he considered to be the most precise value for the Old Kingdom cubit, from the carefully measured dimensions of the carefully constructed rose granite King's Chamber in the Great Pyramid:

"If a strictly weighted mean be taken it yields 20.620 ± .004 ; but taking the King's Chamber alone, as being the best datum by far, it nevertheless contracts upwards, so that it is hardly justifiable to adopt a larger result than 20.620 ± .005" (Petrie 1883: 179).

This gives the length of the cubit as **523.748mm** ± 0.127mm, and so accords with the other sources.

Other scholars warn however that: "Their lengths (surviving cubit rods) vary from 52.3 to 52.9 centimetres, reminding us that ancient measures were not so standardised as those of today and that such discrepancies have to be taken into account in our calculations of Egyptian buildings" (Arnold 1991: 251).

Nevertheless, Petrie notes the rigorous consistency maintaned during the the Old Kingdom, and that "There are no examples of the measurement instruments of the early dynasties, when extreme accuracy was attained" (Petrie 1940: 68).

We can see from the figures for Saqqara and Giza (524mm and 523.75mm), that the cubit [Figure 10] was already impressively accurately applied from its earliest attestations in the third and fourth dynasties, but the consistency with which this size was maintained over time is also impressive, and many rules have been found from centuries and even millennia later of almost exactly this length. Some individual rules do show a notable divergence, and it is thought that some ceremonial rules were not even intended to be used practically at all, and were not made to the standard size. Substantial expansion, contraction and erosion is also to be expected in artefacts of this great age. Nevertheless, from the dimensions of important and well-preserved buildings, such as the Pyramids of Giza or the Temple of Karnak, the evidence shows that the enforcement and preservation of the length of the standard cubit was adhered to closely through the centuries, although some slight variation occurred toward the end of the New Kingdom, and especially into the first Millennium B.C. (Carlotti 1995) when a complete reform was carried out.

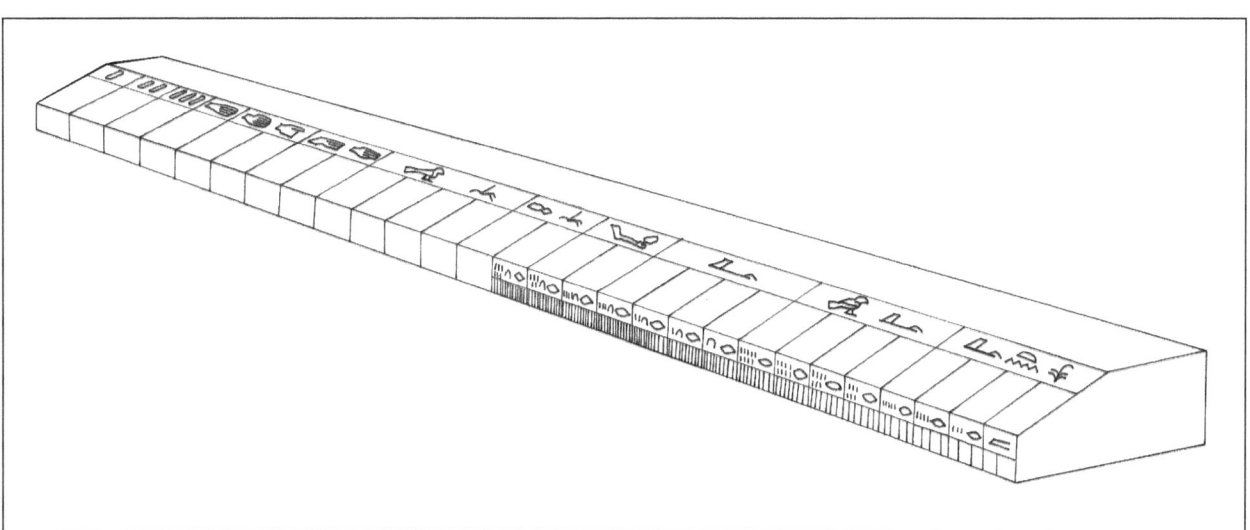

Figure 10 Diagram of cubit rod showing usual divisions and fractions

Chapter 1.   Fundamentals of Old Egyptian mathematics and architecture

From the Middle Kingdom many examples of ceremonial rules are known. Each digit on the rules was also often connected to a particular 'nome' (pronounced nomay), or district of the country, and the symbols of the regions were often drawn on the face of the more elaborate cubits. Once Egypt had been 'united' in the early dynastic period, perhaps under the Pharaoh Narmer, it was subdivided from Aswan in the south to the Mediterranean Sea in the north, into 'nome' districts, each with a central governmental seat, usually a temple, and a 'nomarch', or head of the district, to use the Greek terminology. Although it varied, there were 22 nomes in southern Upper Egypt, reaching from around modern Cairo to Aswan in the south, a distance of around 850 km by the Nile, and 20 nomes in the delta of Lower Egypt, with a perimeter of around 650 km. These vast regions and disparate areas had to be kept together under one united government to ensure peace and stability on the Nile, and much of the governmental iconography of the early dynastic period became obsessed with ensuring a united populace. The multi-layered artistic ideology they developed was so successful that it endured for thousands of years. On one of the more decorative and ceremonial cubit rules the symbols representing the nome regions were included on the upper face. The 22 nome districts from Upper Egypt were drawn onto the first 22 digit subdivisions on the rules, however, as there are more nomes than digits, the first 6 nomes from Lower Egypt were added on the front to match up with the normal 28 digits, and then the remaining 14 nomes were detailed on the otherwise undecorated reverse of the cubit. The standard cubit served to facilitate communication between people of disparate regions, and therefore encouraged social hybridization, and so it is interesting to note that the iconography on the cubits also acted to unite people symbolically. We can see a certain logic to including the emblems of the regions that used the cubit on the rules themselves. This served to unite the people symbolically, and literally, under one ruler.

Another cubit mentions a 'house of the royal cubit', possibly in the Memphite nome region (Scott 1942: 73). It is tempting to think of this as the central storehouse for a cubit standard, or the official home of the scribes responsible for enforcing standardised weights and measures. Something akin to this actually exists beside the temple of Karnak in Upper Egypt, where a small 'sed festival' monument, built during the reign of pharaoh Sesostris I who lived c.a. 2000 B.C., is found. This finely built and now reconstructed kiosk, known as the 'white chapel', which is one of the oldest surviving structures at Karnak, was decorated in a way very similar to a ceremonial cubit rod, with digits and fingers and the associated iconography shown across the southern façade. Additional measurement related information regarding the nome regions was also displayed, including the surface areas of each nome, and the heights of the inundation in each region of Egypt (Lacau and Chevrier 1969; Lamy 1991: 76).

Each digit was also allocated a different god, from Re at digit one, through Shu, Tefnut, Geb, Nut, Osiris, Isis and Seth and so on. The tiny lines along the lower edge of the rule (below) also show that the digits themselves were finely subdivided. Unlike our modern rules, which have each centimetre subdivided into an equal ten millimetres, the Egyptian digits were each divided into different fractions, from one half on the first digit, then into thirds, then into quarters, right up to sixteenths, as is shown on the front of the rule in the photo below [Figure 11]. This was probably a result of their 'difficult' unit fraction system, which will be discussed later, whereby larger fractions were built up from lots of smaller unit fractions, so that our 'three quarters', for example, could only be expressed by adding together 'one half and one quarter', by the Ancient Egyptians.

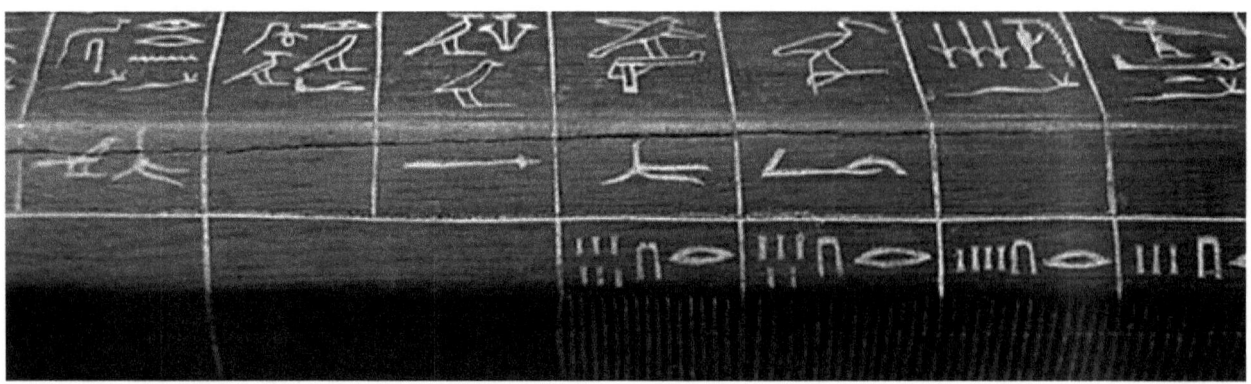

Figure 11 Close up of the scale of an 18th dynasty cubit rod of Maya

The ability to communicate standardised information about raw materials and agricultural produce between population centres up and down the length of the Nile must have been one of the ways in which the disparate regions were kept together, and the standardised measurement systems must have been a vital factor in facilitating and even encouraging trade, communication, and by extension, the unification of Egypt as a whole. In many ways the standardised royal cubit underpinned the economy and the cohesion of Egypt. This quantum leap development of a standardised measurement system perhaps goes some ways towards explaining the rapid

Chapter 1. Fundamentals of Old Egyptian mathematics and architecture

development and extraordinary speed with which Old Kingdom Egyptian civilisation flourished.

Given the historical significance of this measurement system it is surprising that no comprehensive study has ever been compiled or published that discusses all of the surviving rules and textual evidence in one place. Even in 1942, Scott of the Metropolitan Museum of Art wrote "A group of Egyptian antiquities which has never been satisfactorily studied is that of the "ceremonial cubit rods." (Scott 1942: 70). Many excellent publications have addressed individual rules or even several rules at once, but no attempt has been made to develop a definitive guide to the Egyptian cubit.

Useful publications that can be referenced or included in any future compilation would include: (Bey 1878; Petrie 1926; Scott 1942; Ioppolo 1967; Gillings 1982; Dilke 1987; Dekoulakou-Sideris 1990; Carlotti 1995; Ebeling and Meissner 1999; Lepsius 2000; Petit 2000; St. John 2000; Lightbody 2008), but the reader is forewarned to be extremely judicious regarding other works on this subject in general. A huge number of flawed publications are in circulation that present inaccurate information regarding the cubits as fact. Some of the reasons for this are discussed in Appendix 2.

Figure 12 A Middle Kingdom model of a typical Egyptian Granary

The royal cubit measurement system is known fully developed into 28 parts from at least as early as the building of the first Step Pyramid at Saqqara, and the standard system possibly predates even this, with cubit glyphs appearing on some late predynastic ceremonial palette decoration.

As well as facilitating the development of an agricultural economy, measurement also allowed architecture to be designed and stone to be quarried to planned and regular sizes. It is around the second or third dynasty, just before the pyramids first evolved, that we see the development of the first cut stone masonry. Rather than being a development based on older megalithic rough-stone building methods, it seems the first stone buildings in Old Kingdom Egypt were built from regular small cut blocks of stone based on their mud brick precursors. Continued use of mud brick arrangement techniques in the lithic medium, such as in the arrangement of 'headers and spreaders' in wall construction, supports this. Examples from the Reisner Papyrii (Gillings 1982: 219) show mathematical problems calculating temple excavation workloads, the workforce required and volumes of stone

Chapter 1.   Fundamentals of Old Egyptian mathematics and architecture

to be ordered from the storehouse, listed by length, breadth and height as well as total volume.

Symbolically, the royal cubit was much more important than just a technical system, and it played an important role within the temple based cosmology of the country.

This may be difficult for us to appreciate in an age when technical systems and religion have been largely separated, but it is important. Extensive analysis of the symbolism on the ornate ceremonial rods, some made from solid granite and carved with hieroglyphs, shows just how much importance was placed on these rods, yet their function was ultimately a practical one (Scott 1942).

The length of the standard royal cubit was first derived archaeologically from analysis of the dimensions of standing architecture in Egypt. Mainstream Egyptology has accepted the basis of this process for more than a century, and there is widespread acceptance of the standard length that has been re-established by the archaeologists and Egyptologists involved in the recovery of architectural data.

In 1865, Richard Carl Lepsius, the famous German Egyptologist wrote: *"The most likely occurrence of dimensions with a round number of cubits might be expected to be found in rooms, such as the funerary chambers inside pyramids, and there is no doubt that this assumption is right in many cases. The true situation will reveal itself if we collect the measured dimensions of such rooms and reduce them to the length which appears most probable for the cubit, **0.525m**."* (republished Lepsius 2000) [my emphasis].

Figure 13 Reconstruction of sculptural workshop. NMS, Edinburgh

Although the value for the length of the cubit that Lepsius derived was very slightly too large, the measurement of funerary chamber referred to here stems from the widely known and accepted fact amongst Egyptologists that the so-called 'Kings's Chamber' of the Great Pyramid was built on a ground plan of precisely 10 x 20 cubits. The dimensions of this cuboid room, finely built in hand quarried blocks of rose granite, transported all the way from Aswan in Upper Egypt, allow us to see, with confidence, the existence, use and application of standardised dimensions in the Old Kingdom architecture of the pyramid age, around 2,550 B.C. In addition, it lets us see that pharaonic funerary construction used massive, measured and valuable stonework ordered, quarried and transported the length of the country, almost 750 km from Aswan to Giza.

Chapter 1. Fundamentals of Old Egyptian mathematics and architecture

Measurement and geometry was certainly being employed spatially in true architectural design even before this, such as in the 'mastaba' tomb 17 at Meidum, which dates to c. 2,700 B.C. (Arnold 1991: 12), where construction instructions have survived, written on the walls in red ink.

The way in which the technical and the religious were intertwined in their world means that a study of their architecture cannot be carried out in isolation from their other cultural systems, even the organised agriculture. More specifically, when the structures in question are pharaonic and funerary in nature, religious traditions play a very direct part in the technical architectural design.

Almost every aspect of pharaonic funerary architecture developed a symbolic role over time, and the way in which the measurement and geometric systems were applied within the architecture was no exception.

With the advent of measured stone construction and a growing workforce fuelled by well-organised agriculture, buildings were created of a magnitude that was previously unknown. As well as having a functional role as defensive structures, many aspects of the new buildings became monumental, and served to support the hierarchy as much through their impressive appearances as through their practical value.

The new buildings served to consolidate the power of the scribes who organised their building, and ensured the continuity and increasing power of the ruling community. The scribes employed all their skills in geometry and arithmetic in the construction of their buildings. Since the Early Dynastic period two types of buildings became the most prominent of these symbols. These were the palaces for the living that continued to be built in mud-brick, and the funerary monuments for the afterlife, now built in stone. The most important building for the afterlife was that belonging to the chief at the top of the hierarchy, the pharaoh.

Figure 14 Reconstruction of the lost sarcophagus of Menkaure

"The royal tomb became the principal public statement on the nature of kingship. Changes in royal tomb architecture are thus our most important single guide to the evolution of ancient perceptions of the monarchy" (Kemp 2005: 99).

Chapter 1. Fundamentals of Old Egyptian mathematics and architecture

The pharaoh was: "...a single king whose power as an earthly ruler was expressed in monumental architecture, in ritual and in symbolic art" (Kemp 2005: 109).

Understanding how these traditional building forms developed and were combined with new ideas and new technologies is complicated, and attempting to find any simple 'master theory' that explains every aspect of the architectural symbolism or can be 'proved' is simply not possible. A more subtle and complex understanding of the gradual step-by-step changes that took place through time is something that can nevertheless be usefully achieved [see Figure 3 for timeline of sites mentioned in text]. Rituals and traditions had to be maintained in royal funerary architecture and the complex way that these restraining forces were synthesised with new technical developments must also be understood. The pharaoh was closely identified with these symbolic buildings to the extent that the living pharaoh's name was even written within a device representing the palace building [Figure 15]. This symbol constituted the royal Horus Name of the pharaoh, as Horus the falcon was always shown either perched on top of or standing beside the symbolic palace containing the pharaoh's title. In death, the pharaoh's funerary monument and the sarcophagus itself were often decorated to represent this 'palace façade'.

Figure 15 Sneferu's Horus name in a Palace 'Serekh' symbol

Old Kingdom sarcophagi were often shaped and decorated just like the mastaba tombs from the earlier dynasties. The reconstruction of pharaoh Menkaure's sarcophagus, lost at sea during transportation back to England in 1838, demonstrates the close relationship between the pharaoh and the royal buildings, both in life and in death [
Figure *14*].

The sarcophagus of Amenemhet III from the Middle Kingdom is another good example of this (Lehner 1997: 180), and also shows the vaulted roof often seen covering the mastaba tombs. Even the word pharaoh originally referred to the 'great house', 'pr aA', which was the official palace, and this word was only used for the actual person from the Middle Kingdom, and most notably from the Amarna period of the New Kingdom, onwards (Griffith 1901). Dynastic rule, the pharaoh and the royal buildings were therefore intimately related in life and in death.

Just as their stone tomb structures developed from the simple 'mastaba' mounds through to step pyramids and on to true pyramids through time (Kemp 2005: 112), their mathematics, arithmetic and measurement systems simultaneously developed in sophistication and complexity, and all of these processes must be understood together, within the one cultural context.

As well as the technical and bureaucratic aspects of an Ancient Egyptian scribe's life, there were also rather more exciting and mysterious aspects. Royal rituals and superstitions regarding the gods and the afterlife were profoundly important, and were described and recorded in detail. These religious aspects, many of them with far older roots, were considered extremely powerful forces at the time, and as there was no clear line of separation between religion and technical matters as we have today, there were certainly many crossover points.

Rather than abandon the old gods and traditions when the new era of literacy and architecture began to emerge, the scribes simply combined them with the newly developing technologies to produce novel and more formalised expressions of much older ideas (Kemp 2005: 112).

The rapid technical developments of the Old Kingdom pyramid builders relied on a combination of bureaucracy and religious tradition to manage and organise the people, and what these combined forces produced from a technical, architectural and physical point of view was certainly dramatic and was surely exciting to experience at the time.

The dimensions of the pyramids on the Giza Plateau near modern Cairo allow us to see how the geometry of the Old Kingdom scribes was applied in their symbolic monuments, but only if the dimensions and architecture are interpreted within the context of ancient Egyptian mathematics, and that means with reference to the Royal cubit.

Although the tombs and pyramids of Egypt are undoubtedly enormous geometric forms, they played a much more integrated and symbolic role in the evolution of Egyptian culture. As an on-going construction project involving thousands of people, the royal tombs served as a venue for people to work together, communicate and integrate with one another, as well as being visual symbols of this unification process. The efficient organisation of Nile agriculture, with governmental taxation of surplus food production, eventually allowed building projects to be undertaken on a huge scale. At the same time, the cyclical nature of the Egyptian year, with its floods and dry seasons, was particularly conducive to an annual building season devoted to re-enforcing and re-

Chapter 1. Fundamentals of Old Egyptian mathematics and architecture

stating the Pharaoh's legitimacy to rule the entire united country (Kemp 2005: 99).

At Giza, the factors determining the differences and similarities seen between the funerary structures, including the three royal pyramids, are many and varied. The reasons for the particular choice of locations for each pyramid, and the relative positions of them, have remained a matter of enthusiastic speculation for many centuries. It is only in the last few years that serious and systematic efforts have been made to explain the decisions taken by the Egyptian rulers and architects in a more academic way, and with reference to their culture, religion, technologies and traditions [Figure 16]. Aspects of landscape archaeology have also become prominent recently, and can be applied usefully at Giza, where practical concerns due to the terrain available were certainly influential, as will be discussed.

Nevertheless, ritual, symbolism and tradition also played a major role in determining pyramid location choices on the site. In fact, as one studies the factors that were considered, it becomes apparent that many different issues were of importance, and that the symbolic and practical concerns relating to the site were all inter-related.

Figure 16 The Louvre Scribe from the Vth Dynasty

This sort of multi-layered symbolism is something that is seen widely in early Egyptian material culture and iconography, and in the culture as a whole. It is possible that this multi-layering of ideas was in part a hangover from pre- and proto-literate Egyptian society. In a community without paper or records, preservation and communication of information would have been carried out through people's living memories, and in conjunction with the changing ritualised landscape and traditional materials and myths, rather than as issues recorded on paper in isolation from a wider context.

The way in which we subdivide, categorise and record knowledge systematically today seems quite normal, but in the past it may have been more usual to integrate important knowledge with reference to existing traditional symbolism. As a result of this older method of information communication, older traditions heavily influenced the iconography and theology of the new dynastic Egypt, despite the importance of the new technical developments and growing literacy.

Chapter 1. Fundamentals of Old Egyptian mathematics and architecture

It is well known that the multi-layering of different ideas enables them to be memorised more easily, so that it is possible that the complexity of symbolism observed in the Old Kingdom iconography was a characteristic of pre-literate society.

The intertwining of practical and religious concerns is one of the reasons that the Giza site, and other sites of Old Kingdom Egypt, are so fascinating to study, and difficult to interpret. This may also be the reason why people today are so ready and able to project their own technical and religious ideas back onto the site, adding yet more layers to the multi-layered ideology associated with this ancient project. Nevertheless, we now have to hand enough evidence and data to finally synthesise the architectural, archaeological, cultural and textual evidence into one historical narrative.

The royal cubit was an integral part of the early state development that assisted the expansion of industrial scale agriculture, the growth of the administrative class of scribes [Figure 16], surveyors, tax collectors, overseers of surplus, and the evolution of monumental architecture.

The architecture that it enabled symbolically legitimised the centralised pharaonic rule that kept the country unified, and so underpinned the stability of the society.

Standardised measurement became part of the monumental, architectural, pharaonic preservation system.

As noted, there is no record of when or why the standardised measurement system that was the royal cubit was subdivided into its curious 7 parts, but there are several natural characteristic of this setup that strongly suggest that the reason was linked to the cultural context in which it first developed, and to facilitating practical problem solving.

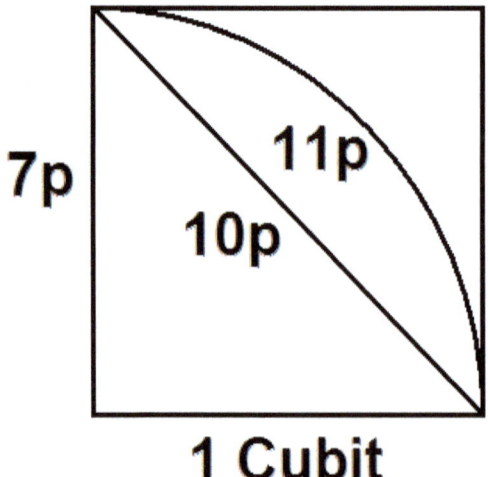

Figure 17 Basis for the 7-palm cubit: diagonals and circles made easy

The important diagram above shows how the 7 palm cubit is particularly well suited to measuring out square diagonals as well as circular circumferences. Neither of the approximations in the middle of the square is exact, but the diagonal is very close to being exactly 10 palms (only 1.02 % from being the true length of the diagonal), whilst the quarter-circumference is almost exactly 11 palms (only a tiny 0.04% in error from being the true length of the quarter circumference). This means that the circumference of a full circle, swept out by a 7 palm cubit, is very precisely 44 palms in length.

In fact, a 7-part subdivision of the cubit is the **only** number of subdivisions (i.e. into 4 or 5 or 8 or 9 etc) of a rule that can offer approximations of this total accuracy, until we reach 14 subdivisions, which is simply the 7 doubled up again.

From textual evidence we know that the Egyptians were indeed occupied with geometry related to square and rectangular diagonals, and measuring square areas and circular structures, so it is quite plausible that the 7 palm subdivision was a conscious and deliberate choice based on the useful approximations that fall naturally to this setup. Calculations involving circular granary capacities and cuboid block volumes, for example, are known from the mathematic papyri.

Squares and square roots were certainly calculated by the Egyptians by the time the Rhind Papyrus was written (Gillings 1982: 214), and the diagonal of a square was used so often that it was even allocated its own name which was the 'double remen', the remen being the half diagonal (Gillings 1982: 208).

From the simple diagram above [Figure 17], we can see that the quarter circumference of a 7 palm cubit is almost exactly 11 palms, when a right angle is swept out, and so a full circumference is 44 palms. Given the widespread use of the cubit and its application to geometric problems including circular calculations, it seems highly likely that the 7 palms were closely related to facilitating approximations of circular circumferences and square diagonals.

It is also interesting to note at this point the circular symbol of the god Re which is almost always assigned to the first digit of the royal cubits [Figure 18]. This was the case when the symbols for the pantheon of Egyptian gods were included alongside the digits on the rules as 'finger protectors'. The clear association of this circular symbol for the major Egyptian solar god certainly fits with a royal cubit system that originated with respect to circles as well as linear measurement.

When we look at the pharaonic funerary architecture in the following chapter, we will also find clear evidence of circular proportions being applied into rectilinear buildings. Not only that, but the relevant numerical multiples of royal cubits associated with circular forms, 44, 22, 7 and 11, are measurable and observable within

Chapter 1. Fundamentals of Old Egyptian mathematics and architecture

the structures, to an extremely high degree of accuracy, time and time again.

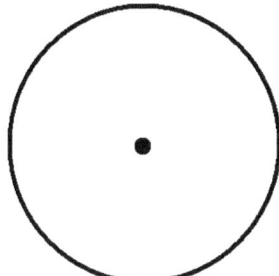

Figure 18 Symbol of the sun god Re from digit 1 of the royal cubit

It was these characteristics of circular proportions and their arithmetic relationships, first found in the Great Pyramid, that first stimulated serious interest in the geometry of the pharaonic monuments.

Nevertheless, it was not until 1883 when the first accurate theodolite survey of the plateau was carried out, by the grandfather of Egyptology, William Matthew Flinders Petrie, that the 'true facts of the matter' started to become apparent.

The next chapter outlines the facts of the matter, as they have been uncovered from pharaonic funerary architecture.

Chapter 2. The evidence and facts of Egyptian circular proportions

2. The Evidence and facts of Egyptian circular proportions

"The science of observation, of registration, of recording," wrote Petrie, "was as yet unthought-of of; nothing had a meaning unless it was an inscription or a sculpture." (Cottrell 1956: 201)

Now that we understand the basic systems of construction and measurement that the Ancient Egyptians used, we can examine the architecture and interpret the design concepts that were deliberately expressing therein.

This chapter summarises the clearest examples of the use of circular symbolism in Egyptian funerary architecture. The intention is not to demonstrate any 'universal law' of Egyptian architectural design, or to prove that any one proportion was applied in every pharaonic tomb. It is only intended to show clearly that an important architectural and cultural tradition, related to the building of royal funerary structures in particular, was developed and variously applied in several different but related funerary contexts. Only by examining each case individually, as well as in comparison with the others from a similar cultural context, can it be seen how the symbolism developed in a logical fashion with respect to the wider architectural and pharaonic traditions, and the technical and artistic skill base. As the actual construction methods used to build the mastaba tombs and pyramids of Egypt have already been discussed at length elsewhere (Arnold 1991; Clarke and Engelbach 1991; Smith 2004), they will not be discussed here. Also discussed at length elsewhere is the projected workforce and organisation required to build a pyramid of the magnitude of what is seen at Giza. The section here has therefore been deliberately restricted to addressing only the symbolic aspects of the architectural designs rather than the physical methods of construction.

The discussion may at first seem data heavy or complex to those not used to handling geometry or measurement data, but in fact all of the examples are directly applied geometry that should be familiar to anyone with a high school education. Most of the examples show that the structures were normally built in clear multiples of whole numbers of the royal cubit measurement unit, so that it should be possible for any Egyptologist, amateur or professional, to follow the discussion. As usual, a basic knowledge of conversion factors between units, and a basic knowledge of conventional notation is useful, such as knowing that 1" = 1 inch = 2.54cm, and that 1 cubit is generally taken as 0.523m or 0.524m, which is 20.61".

As can be seen from Giza, the limits in terms of the magnitude of construction were pushed to extreme levels, but while the designs were new, they were new expressions of traditional forms, and traditional pharaonic symbolism.

This section will detail six separate examples where the traditional circular symbolism was applied in pharaonic tomb architecture. Each case is detailed with a diagram that attempts to convey how the symbolism was applied, as clearly as possible, with references provided to the sources of survey data that were consulted to obtain the facts. Each example will conclude with a short discussion of the cultural context of each case studied.

These six cases are only the most obvious examples of the use of the symbolism, and are covered here only because high quality survey data and dimensions are available for each one. Other probable cases exist, as will be mentioned later on, and it is important to stress that these six main cases are not just a small sample of cherry picked examples, but are the most secure examples, based on the best data available, that can be accepted with a high degree of confidence, and verified if necessary.

Finally, although some very brief cultural context for the architecture is given in each case, this section is primarily concerned with presenting the raw architectural data and the dimensions of the monuments from the survey reports in the most concise manner possible. More in-depth discussion of the actual meaning of the symbolism is reserved for chapter three, while in-depth discussion of the wider cultural contexts of the monuments is already widely available in excellent works published elsewhere (Edwards 1979; Arnold 1991; Lehner 1997; Wilkinson 2000; Verner 2003; Kemp 2005; Schafer 2005).

Chapter 2.   The evidence and facts of Egyptian circular proportions

2.1.   Example 1: Saqqara - around 2750 B.C.

"In the desert, at the edge of the Libyan plateau facing the cultivated land and the picturesque palm groves that cover the few scattered remains of what was Memphis, the capital city of Old Kingdom Egypt, lies Saqqara, the centre of an immense necropolis" (Lauer 1976: 11). This area is where pharaohs of Egypt were buried for the eternal afterlife, but one pharaoh, Djoser, with his architect Imhotep, constructed here a quite new type of monument, the first great pyramid.

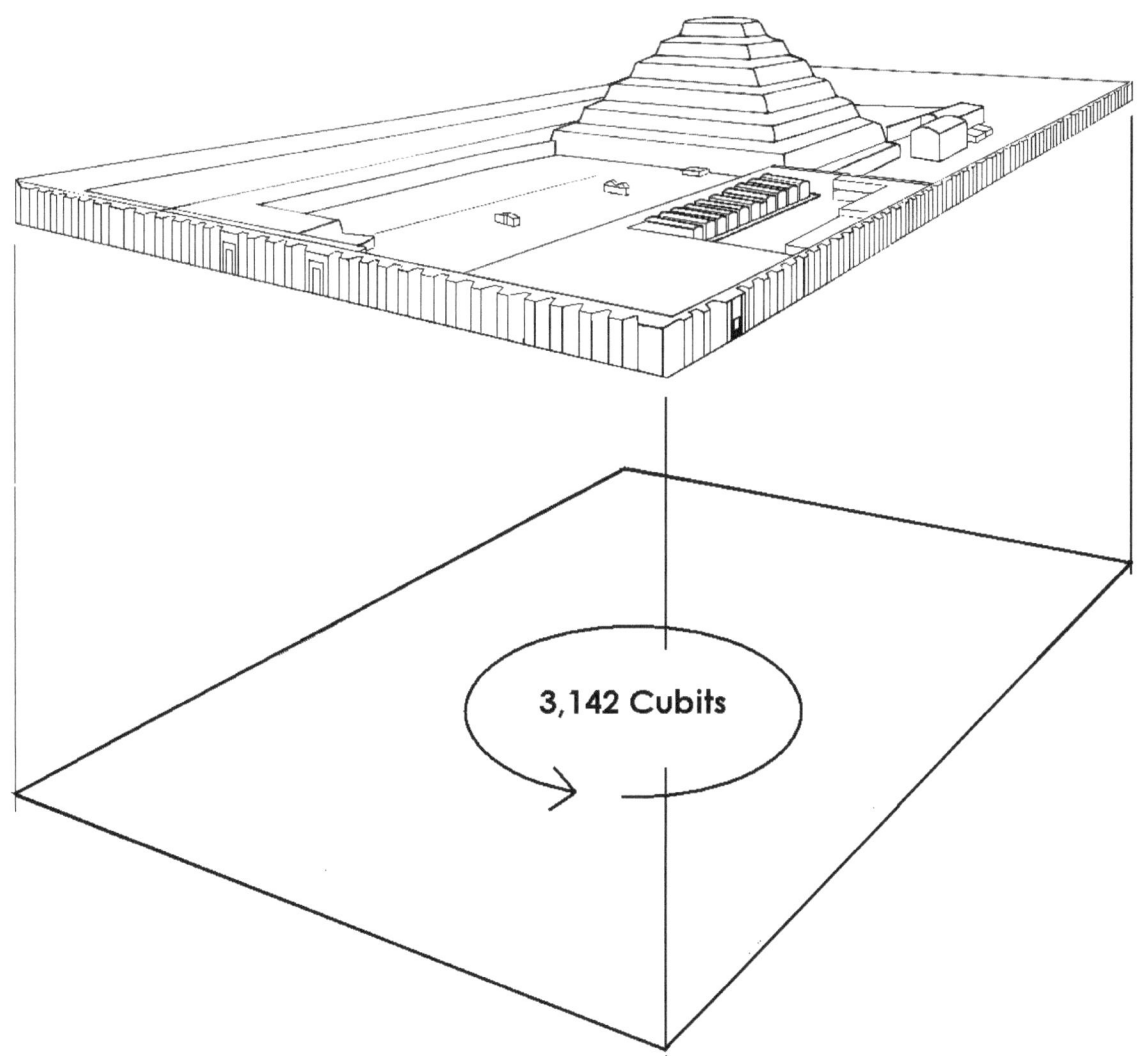

Figure 19 Saqqara Step Pyramid complex with its temenos perimeter

Most importantly for this study, an enormous and continuous perimeter wall, often referred to as a temenos wall, surrounded the pyramid and served to defend and define the protected sacred compound [Figure 19]. In its final form this wall was a work of art in its own right, and was decorated around its four external sides with the traditional regal patterns of stone built niches called the 'palace façade' style. Egyptologist Miroslav Verner gives 544.9m X 277.6m as the external dimensions of this enclosure, with the height of the walls being 10.5m (Verner 2003: 461). Kemp gives 545m x 278m (Kemp 2005: 103). In the original excavation survey report, the French architect J.P Lauer seems to have measured the temenos perimeter wall length to be 544.8m by 276.85m (Lauer 1931: 60), but in the figure quoted below from 1960 he used 544m x 277m.

These different sources give total perimeter lengths as variously:

1642m	(Lauer 1960: 2)
1643.3m	(Lauer 1931: 60)
1645m	(Verner 2003: 461)
1646m	(Kemp 2005: 103)

From these figures it may look uncannily like the wall is in fact getting slightly longer over time, but this seems to have been due to repeated small errors from rounding and copying of data, and repeated conversion between different units of measurement. It serves as a good reminder of why 'primary sources' are to be preferred for the archaeologist.

Chapter 2. The evidence and facts of Egyptian circular proportions

All of these marginally different perimeter lengths are nevertheless equivalent to the circumference of a circle diameter 1000 cubits, which is equal to 3,142 cubits = 1644m, to a very high degree of accuracy (better than ±0.2%). The arithmetical mean of the four modern perimeter length measurements given above is in fact 1644.07m, to an accuracy of 1cm.

In light of the accuracy of this perimeter value and the extensive supporting examples and evidence that follows, it is suggested that this was the deliberate constructional choice made by the Old Kingdom architects for traditional symbolic reasons. These circular proportions, expressed in rectilinear architecture, were associated with pharaonic funerary monuments, and in this case they managed to express the circular symbolism with impressive accuracy for such a grand scale. The underlying meaning of the circular symbolism is discussed in chapter three.

Lauer additionally noted that the overall interior north-south length of the enclosed space was a possibly significant and associated 1000 cubits in length (although he did not relate this to circular symbolism himself). This of course would be the diameter of the circle that is equal in length to the perimeter wall, so that there seems to be a connection between the length and the perimeter of the compound, and the proportions of a circle were apparently the design principle expressed.

Lauer proposed that if the interior length had been deliberately designed to be 1000 cubits, then with a wall width designed to be 20 cubits at either end of the enclosure this gives a total of 1040 cubits for the exterior length, which is 544.4m. This is within half a metre of the actual value measured, which suggests that these were indeed the intended dimensions (Lauer 1931).

By way of refuting that these proportions were actually planned into the structure in this way, it has been pointed out by some sceptics that the sacred walled temenos enclosure was not originally this size during earlier work phases on the site, however, the final structure was certainly completed in this way deliberately, and to these dimensions, and was a continuous and unitary whole. The principal excavator of the site, J.P. Lauer, considered the entire final enclosure to have been modelled on a large early dynastic royal tomb from Naqada in upper Egypt, which is similarly proportioned, but on a smaller scale of 10:1, so that he evidently regarded the completed Saqqara temenos to be a structure that was planned in one event, and which did not randomly evolve by chance.

The palace façaded mastaba at Naqada he identified as a precursor to the Saqqara Step Pyramid complex has traditionally been attributed to Menes, who reputedly first united Egypt, but who is now thought to be a mythical figure. In fact, it dates to the time of king Hor-Aha. The tomb is also now associated with the queen of Hor-Aha, Neithotpe, and although it did not hold a royal burial, it was possibly a cenotaph set up in a significant location. It has a substantial niched palace-façade temenos wall of 1m in thickness surrounding it, and was rectangular in form at 54m by 27m (Baines and Malek 1980: 110). This gives a perimeter of approximately 162m, and an internal length of close to 100 cubits (Spencer 1979: 149; Dorner 1991: 83), something that is echoed by the 1000 cubit internal length of Saqqara, but on a larger scale of 1:10.

If the traditional circular symbolism at Saqqara had been inherited from this earlier and smaller royal mastaba at Naqada, then it should have had a perimeter of close to 164m. This equates to the circumference of a circle of diameter 100 cubits, as opposed to 1000 for the Step Pyramid temenos wall. Continuity of art forms and symbolism in this way, from the early dynasties to the third and fourth dynasties, is widely accepted (Kemp 2005: 112). At present the latest data from this earlier tomb suggests it may have been very slightly smaller than 164m, at 162m in perimeter, but it is certainly worth considering the many architectural similarities that Lauer noted between this and the Saqqara Step Pyramid complex with its great niched wall. It is also worth noting that the cubit may have been less strictly dimensioned in the Early Dynastic periods, so that some small variation is not problematic to such a theory. Other royal mastaba tombs of various shapes and sizes, and walled enclosures, are known from the experimental period before the development of Saqqara, but this tomb manifests the most striking parallels, and should be noted as a possible precursor.

Lauer wrote that: "The idea of a pyramid shaped edifice to cover the royal tomb seems, in particular, to have been due to Imhotep [the architect]. Up to his time the royal funerary chamber and its associated rooms were first constructed more or less at ground level, and then interred at various depths into the ground until its was finally completely underground. It was covered only with a rectangular structure of brick, with its length lying in the north south direction, and decorated with a niched wall, of varying complexity, imitating the exterior appearance of the 'White Walls' of the royal city of Memphis, built by Menes, the unifier of Egypt and the founder of the 1st dynasty. The most well known example of this design is the royal tomb of Naqada that was perhaps the tomb of Menes himself. Imhotep gave to the funerary enclosure of Djoser the dimensions of the tomb at Naqada, but enlarged it by ten times to 544 m x 277 m in place of 54 m x 27 m. It was by way of this rectangular plan and the niched decorative walls that he preserved the character of his ancestors' royal tombs. But, whereas in the earlier cases the different elements were intimately connected by a single structure that covered everything, Imhotep disengaged the tomb itself from its annexes, made it the dominant element, and designed a vast pyramidal edifice, firstly of four steps and then of six. We have been able to establish, from other aspects, that Imhotep did not imagine this concept straight away, because the pyramid covered an earlier structure that had been enlarged twice itself." (Lauer 1960: 2) (translated by the author).

Chapter 2. The evidence and facts of Egyptian circular proportions

In light of this statement regarding the symbolic royal form of the Saqqara perimeter wall, it is interesting to see that Flinders Petrie applied to survey the perimeter wall of Saqqara directly after he had finished his survey of the Giza plateau and its three great pyramids. The survey of Giza was the crucially accurate survey in which he first disproved all of the many radical theories about the size of the Great Pyramid, and also first concluded that the circular proportions he observed there were incorporated deliberately into the architecture and were therefore the real design principle used. It seems likely that Petrie considered the possibility that the earlier temenos wall at Saqqara could also have been significant from a symbolic architectural point of view, and he certainly seems to have been keen to excavate and survey there.

Figure 20 The Step pyramid of Saqqara – the first pyramid

From the 1883 Egyptian Exploration Fund proposal: "In Saqqara, he would examine the peribolus wall of the Step Pyramid to see if it threw light on the date of the pyramid; this would take a week" (Drower 1985: 69).

In fact, Petrie tried time and time again to obtain a permit to dig at Saqqara: "There was one particular concession he now desired above all others: Saqqara, that vast necropolis on the cliff above the ancient capital, Memphis, which had already yielded so many treasures to the spade. Two sites in particular he coveted: the area around the Step Pyramid (was this Zoser's tomb, or had he been buried at Beit Khallâf?) and near the Serapeum where he hoped he might find the burials of the earliest sacred Apis bulls, perhaps from the First Dynasty" (Drower 1985: 272).

But:

"The Archaeological Committee met on 15 November 1903 and refused Petrie permission to dig at Saqqara on any terms whatsoever. …… He was disappointed and angry, and felt that Maspero had let him down; relations between them were never easy afterwards, and once or twice they became distinctly strained."

"Petrie did not ask again for Saqqara; it remained one of the few major sites in Egypt never to have come under his spade."

The Step Pyramid at Saqqara is highly irregular in shape and plan. The base is not square, but rectangular, and the steps are sloped, so that there was probably no real systematic geometry to its form beyond a gradual reduction in size of each step towards the top. The step form is in fact thought to have evolved or developed from the idea of building a sequence of the earlier 'mastaba' type flat top tombs on top of each other [Figure 20].

Although Petrie never had an opportunity to examine the Step Pyramid or its carefully constructed temenos wall in more detail, he did obtain permission to excavate another early great pyramid of the Memphite necropolis, that of Meidum, on the edge of the desert some distance up the Nile.

The results of that research, and the circular symbolism he found there, are detailed in the following section.

Chapter 2. The evidence and facts of Egyptian circular proportions

2.2. Example 2: Meidum – around 2600 B.C.

Although perhaps begun by pharaoh Huni, the pharaoh Sneferu most likely completed the pyramid at Meidum, around 2,600 B.C. He also turned it from a step pyramid into the first true pyramid. By filling in the steps with limestone encasing blocks he created the pyramidal form that is so familiar to us today. The Medium pyramid, however, appears to have collapsed sometime during the New Kingdom, and is sometimes known as the Collapsed Pyramid or the Failed Pyramid as a result. The Egyptologist and surveyor Flinders Petrie was the first to accurately reconstruct its final dimensions, from the survey data he collected in the 1890s during his excavations in the Meidum area (Petrie 1892).

Figure 21 The Collapsed Pyramid at Meidum and fields of the Nile

What Petrie found at Meidum was clear evidence that the original 'as-built' proportions of the pyramid, in its final form, were such that the base perimeter equalled the length of a circumference produced by a radius equal to the pyramid's height.

In this new pyramid complex, in its final form, the temenos wall and the buildings within the temenos court had been greatly reduced in relative importance, and most of the emphasis was transferred to the pyramid itself. Similarly, whereas the circular proportions had originally been applied to the temenos wall at Saqqara, and not to the irregular Step Pyramid, it seems that they were applied directly to the primary dimensions of the regular true pyramid at Meidum itself.

Surveys since then have confirmed these proportions, and also that the actual numerical values of the dimensions in cubits have some archaeological value to us today, as we try to interpret and understand the intentions of the pyramid's Old Kingdom architects.

The actual values Petrie calculated for the dimensions of the completed structure were as follows:

As-built height 92m, pyramid side lengths 144m, pyramid base perimeter 576m (Verner 2003: 461). In royal cubits this is almost exactly 44 x 25 around, and 7 x 25 in height. Petrie suggested that the Old Kingdom architects were deliberately applying the numbers 7 and 44 to the proportions of the monument, on a scale of 1:25. This produced a pyramid with the desired symbolic circular proportions, and of a culturally suitable size for the time, in fitting with the technical developmental sequence, progressing through the third dynasty and into the great fourth (Petrie 1892: 6) [Figure 22].

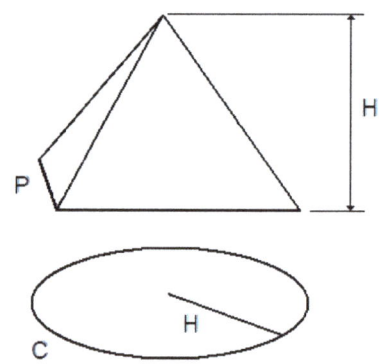

Figure 22 Meidum pyramid with primary dimensions

In other words, they applied the traditional circular symbolism at the largest scale they could physically build at the time.

In the excavation report for Meidum (which he referred to as Medum), after measuring the slope and dimensions of the pyramid, Petrie wrote (using inches as well as royal cubits which is somewhat confusing):

"This angle, it will be seen, is just that of the Great Pyramid of Gizeh, which was built next after this pyramid. And we have therefore to consider if any of the theories concerning the size of that are elucidated by this. Now the most simple and promising theory is that the ratio of 7 : 44, for that of a radius to a circumference, is embodied by the Great Pyramid height being 7 x 40 cubits and its circuit 44 x 40 cubits ; in short, that it was built 7 and 44 times a modulus of 40 cubits. The angle being the same here at Medum the ratio 7 : 44 will of course hold good ; the question is if a simple modulus

Chapter 2.   The evidence and facts of Egyptian circular proportions

was used here also. The base being 5682.0 inches, it is 7 x 25 cubits in height, and 44 x 25 cubits in circuit ; the cubit required being 20.66 +/- .01 inches, or varying from 20.63 to 20.70 according to different sides, which is just the usual range of varieties of the Egyptian cubit. We see then that there is an exactly analogous theory for the dimensions of Medum to that for the Great Pyramid ; in each the approximate ratio of 7: 44 is adopted, as referred to the radius and circle ; in the earlier pyramid [Medum] a modulus of 25 cubits is multiplied by these numbers to fix the dimensions ; in the later pyramid [the Giza Great] a modulus of 40 cubits is used" (Petrie 1892: 6).

To summarise, what Petrie is saying here, it is that the Meidum pyramid was indeed designed so that the perimeter was the length of the circumference of the circle with a radius equal to the pyramid's height. In three dimensions, this produces the now famous side slope angle of **51.842°** in decimal degrees, or 51°50'35" in degrees proper (Lehner 1997: 17), although the Egyptians themselves would not have expressed it in this way as we shall see later.

Compared to Saqqara then, whereas it was the temenos wall around the Step Pyramid that provided the symbolic perimeter, it seems that at Meidum the architects included the circular symbolism within the primary dimensions and proportions of the pyramid itself (Legon 1990). In this way a traditional royal architectural form was combined with the latest technological methods, to produce a new and unique expression of the pharaonic funerary symbolism.

Although the Meidum pyramid was built before the Great Pyramid, Petrie in fact surveyed it after he had surveyed at Giza. This means that it was in fact the older pyramid that confirmed the conclusions he had already tentatively drawn from the later Great Pyramid.

The Meidum survey of 1890 confirmed the conclusions that he had first arrived at on the Giza survey of 1880, and he held these conclusions as given facts for the rest of his life.

The next example shows the key data that Petrie first measured accurately at Giza, and shows how the same symbolic approach was followed by the Old Kingdom architects at Giza during the construction of the first and largest of the three giant Pyramids at Giza, that of the pharaoh Khufu.

Chapter 2. The evidence and facts of Egyptian circular proportions

2.3. Example 3: The Great Pyramid – built around 2550 B.C.

The 'Great Pyramid' west of Cairo in Egypt, the foremost of the giant Giza triplet, was the largest and most carefully built of any pyramid in Egypt. It was built for the pharaoh Khufu, later known as Cheops in Greek. Due to its size and the survival of some well preserved casing stones around its base, it has been possible to reconstruct its original height, base lengths and overall proportions to a high degree of accuracy.

Figure 23 The Great Pyramid of Giza: Wonder of the world for 45 centuries

It is not the intention to discuss the actual construction systems that were required to complete such a massive structure here, but it is worth noting that for almost four millennia it was the world's tallest building, unsurpassed until the 160 metre spire of Lincoln Cathedral was erected c.a. 1300 A.D. Estimates of the workforce required at Giza have fluctuated wildly as more evidence has been put together over the years, but current best estimates suggest that a labour pool of between 20,000 and 40,000 workers was required, with a large unskilled seasonal workforce, who only worked during the flood season, supplemented by more skilled workers who were permanently housed on site. These skilled workers were supplied with everything they needed through the organised surplus collection and redistribution system that was enforced through the royal house, managed by the scribes, imposed from the temples, and produced by the unskilled workforce that spent the rest of the year tending to the fields.

Like Meidum and Saqqara, the Great Pyramid also a temenos wall, and in fact possibly had two, but again, much less emphasis was placed on these walls, which were now merely mud brick and not niched, whereas even greater emphasis was placed on the stone pyramid itself.

Estimates of the total time required to complete the building range from 10 to 20 years, but even at the upper time limit this means that 280 stone blocks of 1500kg each were quarried, roughly shaped, transported to site

Chapter 2.   The evidence and facts of Egyptian circular proportions

and deposited in place, every day, for 20 years, without fail.

The details of this have been discussed at great length elsewhere, whereas this book is concerned only with the true architectural design details, and the incorporation of symbolic aspects through the technical methods developed. As to who was responsible for these design details, the most important historical figure known to have been involved with the Giza project, other than the pharaoh, was the Vizier, or Overseer of Works, Hemiunu. He is often referred to as the architect of the Great Pyramid, but several specialist scribes may have been involved with separate aspects of the design and organisation, so that it is impossible to say who was responsible definitively. Hemiunu was nevertheless certainly an important member of the chief group in charge, and good evidence for this is that he was provided with a very large mastaba tomb just behind the Great Pyramid. Surviving statues of him show a somewhat overweight but authoritative figure with a solid presence.

The actual values for the original dimensions of the building they completed have been measured in great detail, and were as follows:

'As-built' side lengths of the Great Pyramid from Cole's 1925 survey for the Egyptian government (accepted as the most accurate) were:

230.253m,
230.454m,
230.391m,
230.357m, giving an average of 230.36375m (Cole 1925) [Figure 24].

Petrie's earlier 1880 survey data was very slightly different, at:
230.32m,
230.34m,
230.36m,
230.36m, giving an average of 230.345m (Petrie 1883).

The side lengths were therefore extremely precisely laid out, deviating by less than +/-11 cm from the average. Over a distance of more than 230 metres this is impressively consistent by any measure.

The total perimeter length was almost a kilometer, at 921.455m (Cole) or 921.38m (Petrie).

The as-built height has been reconstructed from the archaeological evidence, including the surviving casing stones and core blocks, and is estimated to have been between 146.55m and 146.75m. In standard royal cubits of **0.5235m** these dimensions equate to 1760 cubits around by 280 cubits in height, equalling 440 cubits a side. This gives a height to perimeter of 1760/280, otherwise expressed as 6.2857, or 3.1428 x 2, meaning that the perimeter of the base equalled the circumference of a circle with a radius equal to the pyramid's final height, to an extremely high degree of accuracy. This is exactly the same proportion as at Meidum, but on a larger scale.

It was this level of accuracy in the circular proportions of the Great Pyramid that first brought people's attention to the serious possibility that geometric properties had been deliberately incorporated into the primary dimensions of the monument.

To show how close the correspondence is, if we divide the perimeter length by the height, we have **1760 / 280 = 2 x 3.1428 or 2 x 22/7**. This does not mean the Egyptians used a stand-alone abstract ratio pi in the construction, but it does show that they had highly accurate methods to calculate circumference lengths from radii and diameters.

The mathematical details of this are discussed in the later chapters.

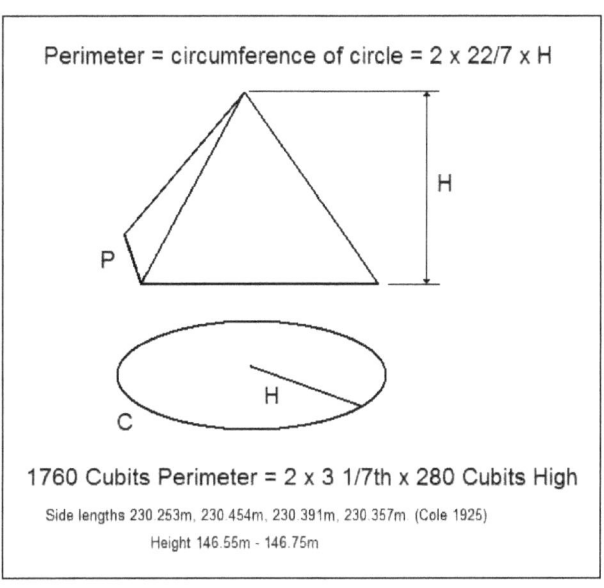

Figure 24 Khufu's pyramid with its primary dimensions

The cultural context and evidence presented in the later chapters confirms that this was indeed the intended reality, and that Petrie's definition of the circular proportions that guided the designs were absolutely correct: *"these relations of areas and of circular ratio are so systematic that we should grant that they were in the builder's design"* (Petrie 1940: 30).

In practice, the slope would probably have been applied to the stone casing during construction through the use of the 'seked' system of angle measurement which is attested in the early Middle Kingdom papyri (Gillings 1982: 184), and which was calculated from the architects' choice of base and height lengths (Legon 1990). In the case of the Great Pyramid the seked would have been '5 palms and 2 digits', so that for every cubit rise, the face slope would retreat 5 palms and 2 digits. This gives the observed slope precisely [Figure 25].

25

Chapter 2.   The evidence and facts of Egyptian circular proportions

From the textual evidence, the 'sekeds' used for applying the slopes on site were calculated from the desired base and height dimensions for any pyramid, and not the contrary as has been suggested. It has been proposed that the slope of the pyramid simply reflected circular proportions because of a coincidence that a seked of 5 ½ gave this slope when a 7 palm cubit was used, but it is in fact more likely that the circular symbolism neatly fits this seked precisely because the 7 palm cubit was originally chosen to facilitate calculation involving circular proportions. This relationship between the cubit and the circle was discussed in chapter one. The relationship means that applied problems of practical circular geometry often fit well into the 7 palm royal cubit system, as well as into the seked slope system.

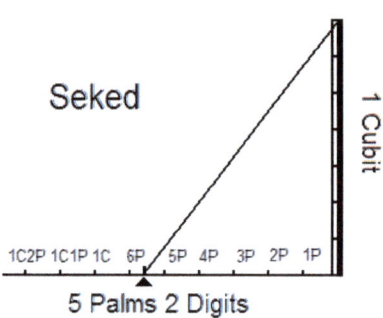

Figure 25 Seked gradient system - slope of Khufu's Pyramid

During the preparation for this book, work was being carried out to verify that the intended proportions and casing stone thicknesses did correspond with what Petrie and other Egyptologists have proposed. A three dimensional digital model of the Great Pyramid was produced in 2007 to demonstrate what the proposed as-built state would actually have looked like.

The diagram below [Figure 27] shows the modern reconstruction based on the highly accurate survey data measured by Flinders Petrie (Petrie 1883), recently reproduced in digital format by long time pyramid researcher and historical reconstruction expert, Jon Bodsworth.

He writes that Petrie's data was ideal for such an exercise as he gives so many measurements as offsets from, for instance, the surrounding stone pavement or other internal elements, and that the modern reconstruction is basically producing a three dimensional version of Petrie's measurements and drawings. Bodsworth used the individual core block layer heights measured by Petrie to build up the pyramid, and was then able to plot the internal elements, and link them where possible with the layer heights. 'Piling up' the individual core layers was straightforward using Petrie's measurements, but putting the casing on was a different matter, as it was necessary to choose which exact measurement to use for the final height, or conversely what precise angle to use.

This is the crucial part of the reconstruction calculation.

Figure 26 Well-preserved casing stones along north face of Khufu

Bodsworth carried out a detailed study of all the surviving evidence, from casing stones [Figure 26] and documentary statements regarding the casing stones. The final 3D reconstruction shown below included his best estimation of the casing stone arrangement based on these, and he was therefore able to calculate the final as-built height of the pyramid from this. He writes regarding estimates of the original height: "As we don't know what tolerances the builders worked to or even the amount of settling etc that might have happened over thousands of years, I think Petrie's stated tolerance of plus or minus 7 inches is still valid and as close as we'll ever get. Even if we knew for certain what method the Egyptians used to establish the height we will never know how close they actually got to it."

The total height he estimates is around Petrie's 5771-5773 +/- 7 inches, or **146.6 metres**, whereas the circular proportions extrapolate to **146.58m** in height (based on an approximation of $3+1/7^{th}$ for the length of a circumference of a circle diameter 1, which equates to the seked of 5 palms and 2 digits), so that the circular symbolism proposal certainly falls accurately within any of the estimated ranges and tolerances.

Again, this equates to the now famous pyramid slope angle of 51.842° in decimal degrees, or 51°50'35" in degrees proper (Verner 2003: 462), although the Egyptians themselves would not have expressed it in this way.

In the author's opinion, the reconstruction by Jon Bodsworth shows the as-built state of the Great Pyramid in a way that is probably very close to its original form and appearance. It is reassuring to know that the reconstruction is based on thorough research, thorough surveying techniques and high quality digital heritage reconstruction technology.

The fine quality of the 'Tura' limestone casing stones, brought down the Nile from the east bank quarries across from Memphis, means that the finished surfaces of the Great Pyramid may well have looked as bright and white as the reconstruction below suggests.

Chapter 2.   The evidence and facts of Egyptian circular proportions

Figure 27 3D reconstruction : - Great pyramid core and casing

In the next section, 2.4, we will see that the same numbers, proportions and dimensions in cubits appear yet again within the most important funerary chamber of the Great Pyramid. In the diagram below showing the internal passages and chambers [Figure 28], the pharaoh was laid to rest in the famous 'King's Chamber' that is shown at the top and to the left of the major passages leading up into the superstructure of the pyramid. In the beautifully built structure of the 'King's Chamber' we again see the symbolic proportions of the circle being incorporated into the rectilinear architecture of a pharaonic tomb.

Chapter 2. The evidence and facts of Egyptian circular proportions

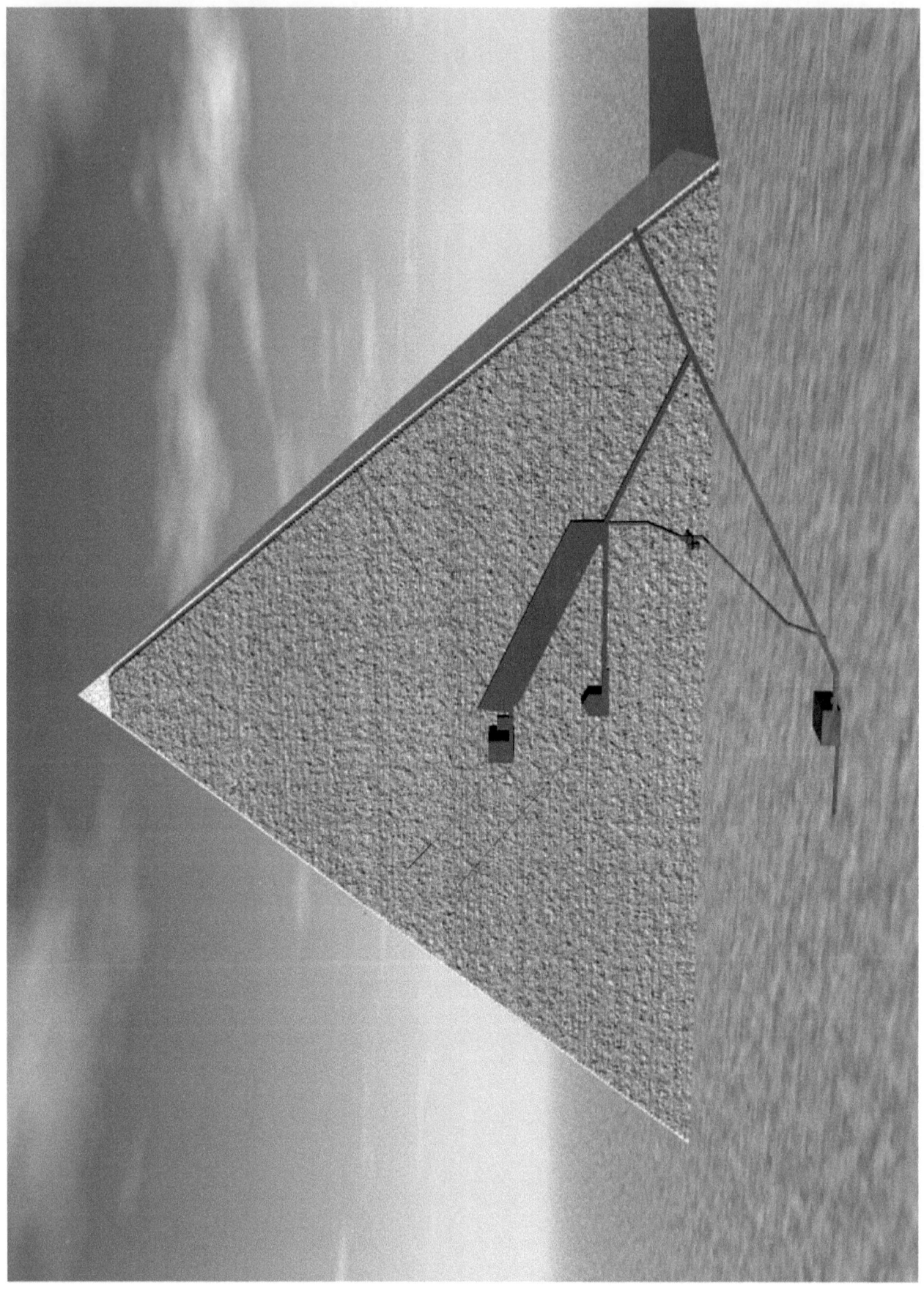

Figure 28 Great Pyramid with interior passages, courses and casing

Chapter 2.   The evidence and facts of Egyptian circular proportions

2.4.   Example 4:   Khufu's King's Chamber walls: around 2550 B.C.

The so-called 'King's Chamber' of the Great Pyramid of Giza is one of the most historically significant locations in the world. A list of the people who have visited this granite-lined space, deep inside the upper structure of the towering pyramid, would include pharaohs, presidents, kings, queens and emperors, as well as millions of tourists from all over the world. Because of the excellent state of the King's Chamber's preservation, measurement of its 'as-built' dimensions can be carried out with a good degree of confidence [Figure 29].

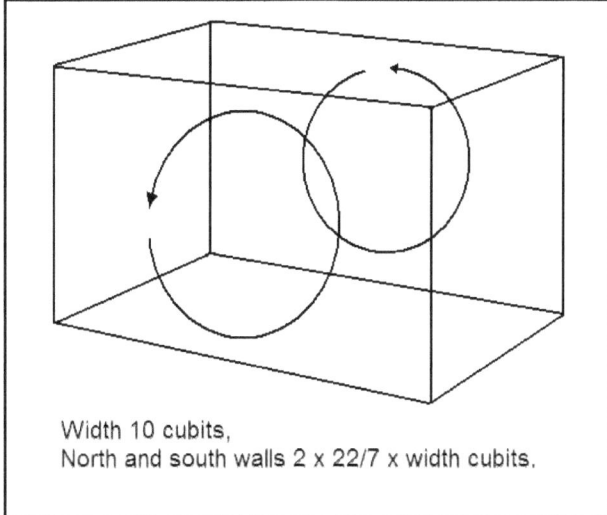

Width 10 cubits,
North and south walls 2 x 22/7 x width cubits.

Figure 29 King's Chamber with its primary dimensions

Petrie writes below, confirming what is shown in the above diagram: *"This same proportion is found in the King's Chamber ; the breadth is the radius of a circle equal to the circuit of the side wall. Here, as the workmanship is very exact, and the length is exactly double the breadth, the height of the chamber is the dimension which makes up the odd amount. Keeping to the old 7 : 11, or rather 7 : 44, proportion, there being 7 palms in the cubit, the radius or chamber breadth is 70 palms, and the side circuit 440 palms. The length top and bottom being 280 palms this leaves 80 for the height."* (Petrie 1940: 29).

The actual dimensions of the room, with the height measured down to the real floor of the chamber, not to the relatively rough surface of paving slabs which is approximately 13 cm thick, are in metres (averaged out across the chamber): 10.47m length x 5.974m width x 5.235m in height (Petrie 1883: 83 and xiii) and (Maragioglio and Rinaldi 1964: Plate 7).

Given the tolerances of 0.6" Petrie quotes, this includes exactly the 80 palms in height that he estimated was the design height deliberately included by the architects, so that the circuits of the north and south sidewalls are indeed 440 palms.

The perimeter circuits of the large north and south walls of the chamber are exactly the same length as the circuits of a circle with a radius equal to the width of the chamber, which is 70 palms wide, whilst the length of the chamber is 280 palms.

We can see here that the same numerical values and circular proportions were applied in the primary dimensions of the King's Chamber as were applied to the external primary pyramidal dimensions and proportions:

External pyramid dimensions – 440 cubits a side, 280 cubits high, equalling radius of perimeter circuit.

Internal chamber dimensions – 440 palm circuit of N & S walls, 280 palm length, width of 70 palms equalling radius of sidewall perimeter circuit.

Due to the construction being from dark rose Aswan Granite, a lithic-type abundantly utilized in pyramid burial chambers, and the fact that the chamber has never seriously failed structurally, it has survived in extremely good condition and in a state that will be very close to its original dimensions. Nevertheless, as Petrie pointed out, the roof is seriously compromised: *"These openings or cracks are but the milder signs of the great injury that the whole chamber has sustained, probably by an earthquake, when every roof beam was broken across near the South side; and since which the whole of the granite ceiling (weighing some 400 tons), is upheld solely by sticking and thrusting. Not only has this wreck overtaken the chamber itself, but in every one of the spaces above it are the massive roof–beams either cracked across or torn out of the wall, more or less, at the South side; and the great Eastern and Western walls of limestone, between, and independent of which, the whole of these construction chambers are built, have sunk bodily. All these motions are yet but small–only a matter of an inch or two–but enough to wreck the theoretical strength and stability of these chambers, and to make their downfall a mere question of time and earthquakes"*

Despite the technical challenges involved, it would seem sensible that given the historical significance of this building, and this chamber in particular, to consider the possibility of undertaking preventative engineering works to improve the stability and strength of the granite roof structure, in order that it survive for future generations to appreciate.

The next section moves out of the Great Pyramid itself and looks at how the symbolism was incorporated across the Giza plateau as a whole. We will look at this by using survey data and three dimensional landscape modelling carried out especially for this study by the author.

Chapter 2.   The evidence and facts of Egyptian circular proportions

Figure 30 King's Chamber and sarcophagus looking west

Chapter 2. The evidence and facts of Egyptian circular proportions

2.5. Example 5: Giza site plan – around 2500 B.C.

J.A.R. Legon first seriously proposed a 'master' geometric plan for the overall Giza site with its three giant pyramids, with all the elements designed and positioned relatively, in 1979. Whilst the reality of the plan as he described it in all its detail is difficult to prove, and is historically problematic in some respects, the overall relative dimensions and extents of the positions of the three pharaonic pyramids (as opposed to the queens' pyramids) were calculated with a great degree of accuracy, and showed an impressive and directly simple geometry that certainly appears to have been deliberately included in the design of the plateau, as it evolved through the fourth dynasty (Legon 1979; Legon 1988; Legon 1989; Legon 1991; Legon 1991) [Figure 31].

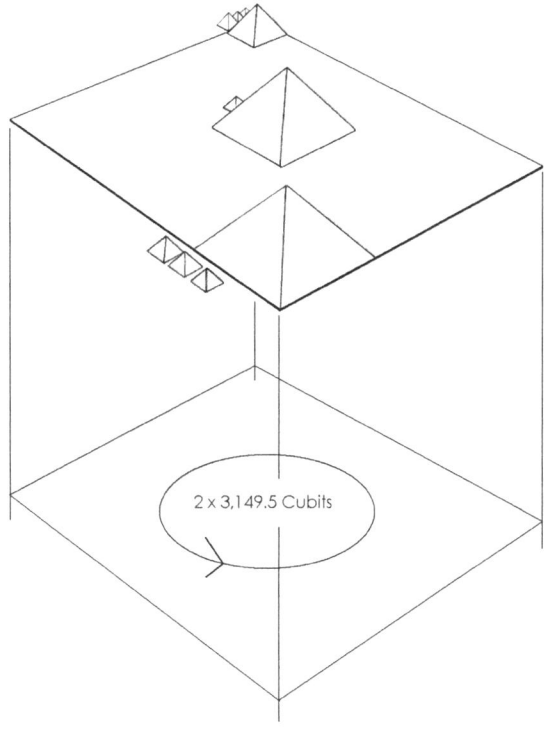

Figure 31 Giza ground plan with primary dimensions

In cubits, Legon found that the north-south length of the rectangle shown in the diagram above expresses the value of root 3 x 1000 royal cubits exactly, while the east-west width of the rectangle is very slightly in excess of root 2 x 1000 royal cubits [Figure 32].

The exact figures he calculated from the theodolite surveys were as follows:

Distance N-S = 1731.97 cubits
Distance E-W = 1417.42 cubits

These side lengths, if they were intended to represent a theoretically ideal rectangle of root 2 x root 3 thousand cubits (1732 x 1417.5 cubits), were only 0.002% and 0.2% in error.

Square roots of 2 and 3 would certainly have been useful and perhaps widely used in Ancient Egypt, as they constitute the side lengths of squares of areas 2 and 3 square units. This would have been useful for doubling or tripling field areas, and there is evidence that a unit called the double remen was effectively a length of root 2 cubits, and was used for this purpose (Gillings 1982: 208).

But why would the Ancient Egyptians have used these root values in particular? And was there a symbolic aspect to square roots as well as for circular proportions?

The answer to this question reveals a crucial aspect of these square roots that is unknown in the modern world today, where only 'absolute' relationships are considered of use or of importance (Rihill 1999: 44). Close approximations are not used, or at least are not taught in mathematics classes, as they are not considered 'high mathematics'. Proofs and pure mathematical relationships are now taught almost to the exclusion of older rules of thumb that were handy for practical reasons. Nevertheless, the cultural context of ancient Egypt suggests that actual practical building and construction was the priority, and so a rule of thumb relationship such as is described below would have been considered useful and perhaps important.

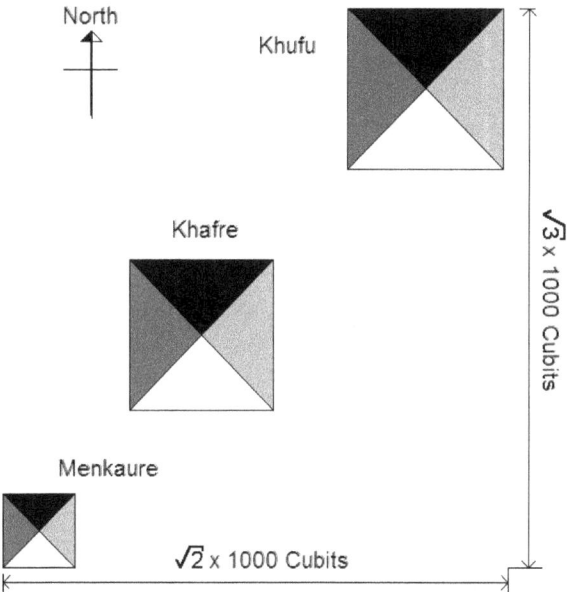

Figure 32 Giza plan with primary dimensions

The 'forgotten' practical relationship that was included here is that root 2 + root 3 equals 3.1462, or almost exactly the length of the circumference of a circle with a diameter of 1 cubit. This means that the perimeter length of the rectangle surrounding the three great pharaonic tombs at Giza is 2 x pi thousand cubits in length, and so again we see the circular symbolism being applied around the royal tombs.

Chapter 2. The evidence and facts of Egyptian circular proportions

There is no real mathematical relevance or value to this close relationship between square roots and pi as described above. It is precise, not exact, but it may have been noticed and perhaps considered relevant by scribes using the 7 palm cubit rules. The numbers on the table below show how good approximations for all these values are available using basic numbers of palms from the seven part cubit. The relationship may have been of some practical use, but from a symbolic standpoint it was considered interesting enough to be incorporated into the architectural design.

Design	Approximation	Difference
root 2 cubits	10 palms	1.00%
root 3 cubits	12 palms	1.00%
pi cubits	22 palms	0.04%
pi	root 2 + root 3	0.10%

Figure 33 Comparison of approximations

Magnifying the root 2 x root 3 rectangle by 1000 times gave the dimensions of the rectangular plan surrounding the three great pharaonic tombs on the Giza plateau. I suggest that this relationship was deliberately included, but only at the time of the positioning of the last of the three great pyramids at Giza, Menkaure's. I do not suggest that this layout was 'pan-generational' or pre-planned during Khufu's reign, as multigenerational planning was not typical. It was an additional layer of the traditional symbolism, adding to the symbolic power of the existing layout, and included only when the position of Menkaure's tomb was being finalised. This means that it was Menkaure's architects who were responsible for the circular symbolism that encompasses the three Giza pyramids when considered together.

Legon correctly identified the square root values of the lengths of the sides of this rectangular layout, but because he did not understand the underlying cultural relevance of the circular symbolism, he was not able to comprehend that the total perimeter length of was in fact the primary dimension of importance, and that the root relationship was only another way of expressing the traditional circular symbolism in an original and interesting way.

Finally, by way of demonstrating further continuity through the dynasties, this Giza plan perimeter, with its circular symbolism, is precisely double the perimeter of the Saqqara temenos wall (+0.2%), so that whereas Saqqara's wall represents the perimeter of a circle diameter 1000 cubits, Giza's plan represents a larger one with a radius of 1000 cubits.

Now that we have reviewed the geometric symbolism expressed in the design of the structures, it is also worth recalling that the actual positions and layout ultimately had to be suited to the landscape requirements that limited the range of choices of the builders [Figure 34].

Rather than constituting an over-arching 'master plan' that dictated every aspect of the design and positioning of the Giza tombs, it is only proposed here that the geometry was one aspect of the multi-layered symbolisms that are seen at Giza, and which were incorporated in pharaonic tombs from the early dynastic mastabas onwards. It is proposed that this circular symbolism was incorporated into a design that was primarily dictated by practical considerations, and only then by symbolic and aesthetic ones.

At Giza the number one factor for determining the position of the pyramids was the landscape topography [Figure 34]. As can be seen from the diagram below (based on data produced by the 'Giza Plateau Mapping Project' directed by Dr Mark Lehner), the three giant pyramids are built along the side of the raised slope of the 'Mokotam Formation' on the usefully and relatively flat platform that forms the eastern edge of the plateau. It is these natural features of the local geology that would have been the primary factor in pyramid location choice.

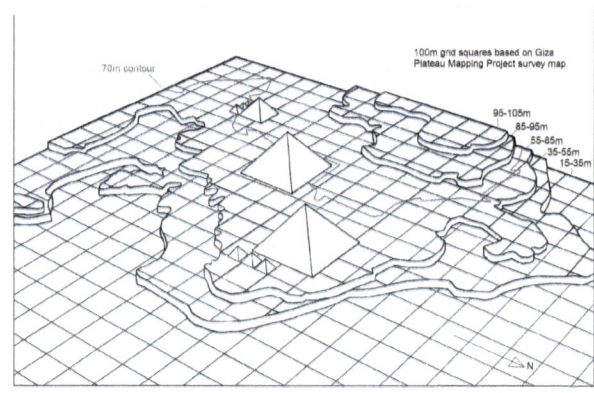

Figure 34 Author's 3D representation of Giza topography

Other practical considerations that influenced design choices would have included proximity to the Nile for the associated 'Valley Temple' causeways, and accessibility for ramps to transport stone to the site. The changing course of the Nile is another major factor that would have been influential in the evolution of the plateau, and this is something that is now being studied in some detail by geologists and Egyptologists (Lutley and Bunbury 2008: 5).

Other symbolic traditions, such as those associated with the pole stars and the rising and setting sun may have been influential, and may have required that clear visibility to the north, east, south and west was available from each pyramid. For religious reasons related to the ascension of the pharaoh's spirit to the heavens, these were all considered important regions of the sky. Aesthetic considerations may also have ensured that the great monuments were built in locations that were visible from the inhabited parts of the Nile, around Memphis and

Chapter 2.   The evidence and facts of Egyptian circular proportions

the apex of the Delta, or from the main existing temples in the region.

All in all, the slightly asymmetrical layout of Giza and the various sized profiles of the great Giza three produces a familiar and pleasing silhouette from most angles, as any traveller on the Nile river or railway will know.

Once the approximate general positions of each subsequent tomb was chosen for practical reasons, the traditional circular and mathematical symbolism focussed on here was incorporated into the precise 'setting out' of the final structure's exact positioning. No preplanning was necessary at the start of construction at the Giza complex, and it was only in the position adjustments of the last pyramid, Menkaure's, that the circular symbolism was finally stretched across the whole site.

Chapter 2. The evidence and facts of Egyptian circular proportions

2.6. Example 6 - Funerary chamber of Amasis II: c.a. 550 B.C.

The final example comes from much later in the Egyptian dynastic era, from the Saïte period, around 550 B.C. In his famous book 'Histories', Herodotus of Halicarnassus, the Eastern Greek travel writer considered to be the 'Father of History', wrote (*Herodotus: Histories: Book II: 175*) "Of all these wonderful masses that which I most admire is a chamber made of a single stone, which was quarried at Elephantine [rose granite], which is twenty days' voyage from Sais. It took three years to convey this block from the quarry to Sais; and in the conveyance were employed no fewer than two thousand labourers, who were all from the class of boatmen. The length of this chamber on the outside is twenty-one cubits, its breadth fourteen cubits, and its height eight. The measurements inside are the following: The length, eighteen cubits and five-sixths, the breadth, twelve cubits; and the height, five. It lies near the entrance to the temple where it was left in consequence of the following circumstance: It happened that the architect, just as the stone had reached the spot where it now stands, heaved a sigh, considering the length of time that the removal had taken, and feeling wearied with the heavy toil. The sigh was heard by Amasis, who, regarding it as an omen, would not allow the chamber to be moved forward any further. Some, however, say that one of the workmen engaged at the levers was crushed and killed by the mass, and this was the reason of its being left where it now stands" (Herodotus. 1996: 191 - 192).

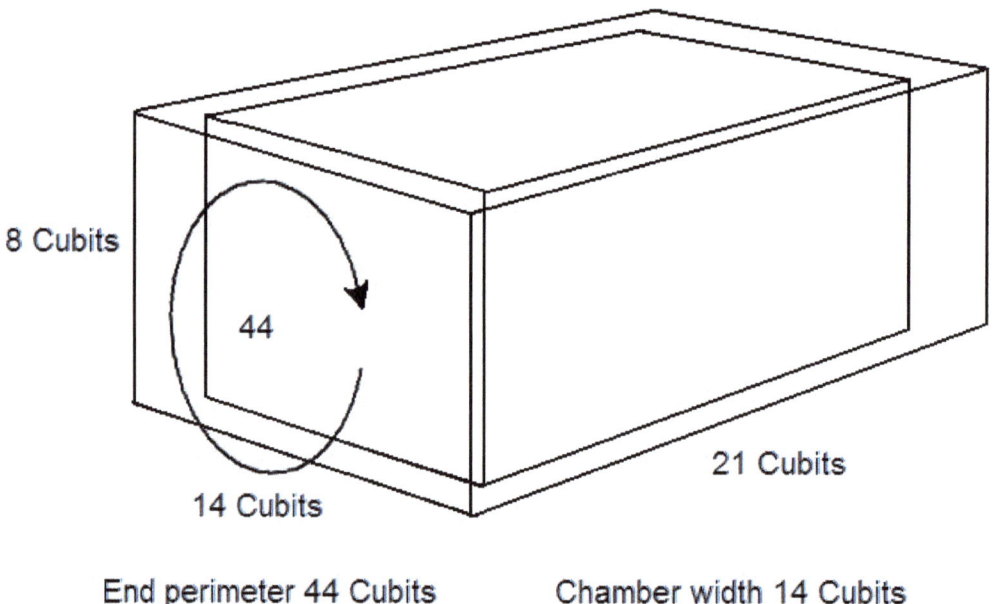

Figure 35 Reconstruction of Amasis's sepulchral chamber

Although this example is from 2000 years after the pyramids were built at Giza, it seems to clearly show the continuity of the application of circular proportions in the pharaonic funerary architecture [Figure 35]. The circuit of the end wall is 44 cubits, while the width is 14 cubits. This means that the width equals a diameter that would produce a circumference equal to the end perimeter circuits.

These numbers expressed in the dimensions, 44 and 14 and 8, are so similar to those seen in the Old Kingdom that it suggests that knowledge of how to include these traditional proportions was passed on right through the intervening centuries. The Great Pyramid's King's chamber had north and south chamber walls of 140 palms in width by 80 in height, giving a total circuit of 440 palms, whereas this chamber of Amasis has end walls of 14 cubits in width by 8 in height, giving a total circuit of 44 cubits.

If this chamber was a funerary chamber as seems likely, then as well as having identical functions, and being made of identical materials shipped from identical locations, these are precisely the same proportions seen in the King's Chamber, and are also the same numbers, expressed at a new scale. This fits well with the cultural context and is another example of how the practical and symbolic criteria that determined the design of the finished tomb were applied by the Old Kingdom architects and builders.

Chapter 2. The evidence and facts of Egyptian circular proportions

This concludes the presentation of the basic architectural data from the 6 case studies. A table summarising the principal dimensions of interest is included on the next page [Figure 36] to allow quick comparison of the relevant proportion. The dimensions are presented in cubits and palms, as these were the cultural context in which the designs were first made, and because the actual numbers of units are relevant, as well as the proportional ratios between different dimensions.

The following chapter now describes what this underlying circular symbolism meant to the Ancient Egyptians, and why they incorporated it within their architectural designs.

Structure Name	Length Height Cubits	Perimeter Cubits	Design Proportion Factor
Naqada Mastaba Temenos	103 N-S	309.5	1 x 3.00
Saqqara Step Temenos	1000 internal N-S	3142	1 x 3.14
Meidum Pyramid	175	1100	2 x 3.14
Khufu Pyramid	280	1760	2 x 3.14
Khufu King's Chamber	70 palms N-S	440 palms	2 x 3.14
Giza Site Overall Plan	Ref Saqqara	6299	2 x 3.15
Amasis Chamber	14 wide	44	2 x 3.14

Figure 36 Tabulated comparison of seven case studies (Factor: 3 significant figures)

Chapter 3.   The Symbolism

3. The symbolism

"...while an understanding of the principles of Egyptian art and of art historical development can begin to help us appreciate the surviving masterpieces, we cannot truly comprehend them without some knowledge of the underlying magic and symbolism intrinsic in their composition" (Wilkinson 1999: 7).

This chapter explores and then explains what the circular architectural symbolism meant to the Ancient Egyptians. In it, I first discuss the various meanings manifested by the circle in Ancient Egyptian art, and then identify which specific form of the symbol was being expressed in the architecture of the royal funerary monuments.

Understanding the traditional religious and ritualistic meanings of the circular symbolism exhibited in Old Kingdom architecture is not a straightforward process. Egyptologists Clarke and Engelbach wrote, as far back as 1930, that the circular symbolism incorporated in the funerary monuments seemed to be present because they were 'sun emblems' (Clarke and Engelbach 1991: 118), but surprisingly little progress has been made regarding this specific issue of meaning since that time. With their statement Clarke and Engelbach nevertheless clearly understood the circular symbolism to be related to the sun. The circle did of course represent the sun in Egyptian art and was often incorporated as part of the winged 'solar disk' emblem. Likewise, the symbol for the sun god Re was a modified form of the circle with a central point [Figure 37]. Nevertheless, the circle as a symbol was not just associated with the sun, and is seen in numerous other roles in the iconographic repertoire that constituted Egyptian religious artwork.

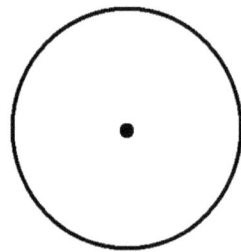

Figure 37 Symbol for the sun god Re

The circle also represented, for example, the Duat, the Egyptian world of the afterlife, when a five-pointed star was drawn within it. It could also represent a star itself, when the circle was shown in red, as carried by a line of gods on Senenmut's astronomical ceiling in his tomb in Deir el-Bahari, but the circle most directly associated with funerary symbolism was the royal 'shen' ring.

The shen ring was a very old, Early Dynastic, symbol in Egypt, and was very closely related to the pharaonic kingship from its first appearance [Figure 38]. A double-coiled rope made up the basic circular shape, with folded ends forming a horizontal bar across its base. A modified, elongated form of this ring also formed the basis for the famous pharaonic 'cartouche' which always surrounded the pharaoh's name, so that the symbol was very closely related to the pharaoh himself. It is thought that the elongation of the shen ring to create the pharaonic cartouche was a direct result of attempting to fit all the hieroglyphs of the pharaoh's name in a line into the looped form, and so its meaning remains unchanged whether in elongated or circular form.

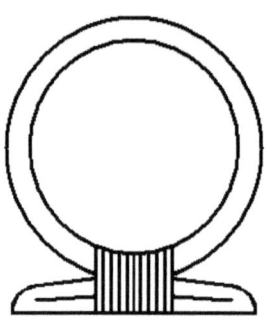

Figure 38 Shen ring

The shen was clearly associated with the life of the pharaoh, but was also associated with mortuary practices and resurrection traditions. For example, the shen ring is often seen as part of the important funerary pectoral necklaces that were wrapped into the layers of cloth used during the mummification of the deceased. In the iconography it is also often associated with the god 'Heh', who recorded the millions of years of unending pharaonic rule on his notched palm fronds [Figure 39].

The shen ring was a device symbolising the protection, longevity and continuity of the pharaonic ruler and pharaonic rule. It was an incredibly important emblem and was directly associated with the life, death and rebirth of the pharaohs. To understand the full meaning carried by the symbol we nevertheless need to review a wider range of examples of its usage in Egyptian iconography, and several good examples are now identified below.

By way of demonstrating the shen ring's association with funerary architecture it is well worth examining Egyptian tombs in general, and not just the pharaonic sepulchres. In later tombs of 'commoners', or at least in those of important but non-royal officials, the shen is often shown as an icon central to the tomb architecture, such in the tomb of Sennedjem, TT1, at Deir el-Medina, where it is shown in a prominent position at the top and centre of the arched end wall [Figure 40].

A pair of enigmatic signs with shen rings also appears on all six decorative panels under Djoser's Old Kingdom Step Pyramid, and on the equivalent panels in the 'south tomb' of the complex. Here the glyph represents half of the hieroglyph for 'sky', and beneath each glyph is the

Chapter 3. The Symbolism

shen ring. These panels at Saqqara are mostly related to the jubilee Sed-festival (HAb sd) when the king renewed his claim over the Egyptian territory, and the Egyptian universe as a whole, after an initial ruling period of thirty years. The jubilee was then repeated every three years after this. During the festival the pharaoh demonstrated his continuing fitness to rule by running around certain symbolic markers, thus laying a renewed claim to his symbolic territory. On four of the panels at Saqqara the Horus falcon, 'Lord of the Sky', is shown flying over the king holding the shen ring, and on the other two panels the falcon is holding the ankh, symbol of life.

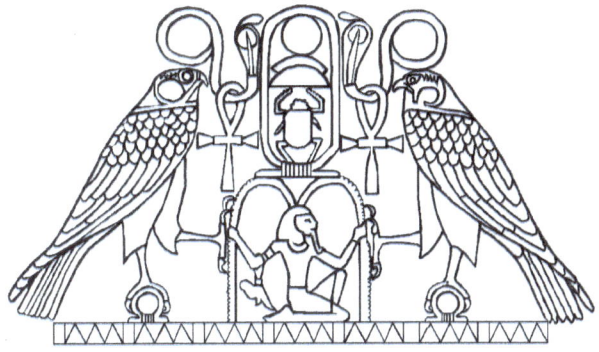

Figure 39 Pectoral necklace of Sit-Hathor-Iunet from c.a. 1870 B.C.

"Some of the panels show Djoser running between the cairns, accompanied by other symbols....Later sources also tell us that the arena itself was called simply 'the field', and the ceremony was called 'encompassing the field' or 'presenting the field', with the emphasis then on the dedication of the arena to a god, although this element is not apparent in the earlier depictions.....It was used as the setting for major royal occasions, such as the reception of tributes, and for a particular ceremony in which the king laid claim to his territory by striding forcefully around its limits" (Kemp 2005: 103).

The general concept seems to be that measuring or marking a boundary, whether it be the boundary of a real field or a symbolic sacred field, could signify taking possession of that territory or designating it as a sacred space. As we have seen in the earlier chapters, boundary measurement with rope stretching was widely used to define and measure areas, particularly the perimeters of any area, whether it was for the all-important fields, or the temple or tomb 'temenos' enclosures, and it was this practice that first necessitated the development of basic geometry. Perimeters were also an important part of the hieroglyphic symbolism used to represent towns, settlements and important buildings from the earliest times in the iconography, and so the fundamental conceptual importance of perimeters needs to be appreciated.

Bearing in mind the importance of perimeters and the delimitation of areas with ropes, the shen, as a double-coiled rope associated with the pharaoh, seems to have represented the idea of designating a territory, or more specifically, defining a sacred and protective space surrounding the pharaoh. As the tradition developed, the iconography evolved so that even when he was outside of a designated secure area he was shown with the shen held above him by the falcon Horus (In later times the vulture goddess Nekhbet of Upper Egypt held the shen), so that the symbol may have encompassed the idea that the pharaoh was protected at all times, whether with boundary walls or by an entourage of bodyguards [Figure 44]. The cartouche and shen are also effectively one and the same symbol, where the cartouche variety had a specific role as a protective boundary surrounding the pharaoh's name at all times [Figure 41].

Figure 40 Tomb end wall shen ring from TT1 at Deir el-Medina

"Shen: Hieroglyphic symbol depicting a circle or ring of rope folded and knotted at the bottom; since the circle effectively had no end, it came to denote infinity. When the Shen sign was depicted encircling the sun, it appears to have symbolized the eternity of the universe. This property of encirclement was extended to denote protection as well as eternity, making the sign doubly potent.........is particularly associated with Horus the falcon or Nekhbet the vulture who hold the sign in their claws above the king, offering him eternal protection......." (British Museum Dictionary of Ancient Egypt 1995: 267)

Figure 41 Cartouches from Abydos Kings list :- Sneferu through Menkaure

Taking an example of the use of the shen emblem from a context almost contemporary with the Giza projects, we can now examine the decoration on the funerary furniture from a reburial of items belonging to Hetepheres, pharaoh Sneferu's wife, found cached at the bottom of a deep shaft to the east of the Great pyramid in 1925-1927 (Lehner 1997: 117).

On the decorative carvings of the wooden canopy, a panel similar to a stele in design shows the falcon holding the shen ring, flying above the Serekh name of the great

Chapter 3. The Symbolism

pharaoh [Figure 42]. The pharaoh's name is spelled out inside the design representing the typical niched palace façade called a 'Serekh' icon. On the top of the Serekh is perched the royal falcon of Horus showing that this is the 'Horus-name' of the pharaoh, which was the official name used when he ascended to the throne during the Old Kingdom. It represents the king as the earthly embodiment of the god Horus, patron of the Egyptian kings. The whole scene sits on a glyph representing the sky, with the 'Was' sceptres, symbols of power, which are usually shown holding up the sky, in this case on either side.

The other typical symbols for authority and longevity surround the palace façade 'Serekh', namely the Djed columns and the Ankhs.

Figure 42 Sneferu's Horus name Neb Ma'at from a royal funerary canopy

The general impression given by this panel, which dates to the correct period of Old Kingdom Egypt, reinforces the proposal that the shen is protecting and empowering the pharaoh.

The pharaonic tomb was, as Egyptologist I E S Edwards (1909-1996) described, regarded as the "Castle of Eternity" of the pharaoh (Edwards 1979: 292). This idea of the tomb as a defensive stronghold for the deceased dovetails well with the idea of the shen ring and solar disc symbolism being incorporated into the geometry and architecture of the tomb structure itself, especially if they were seen as providing protection and empowerment for the pharaoh. In many ways it seems that architectural geometry and mathematical numbers were being used as artistic symbolism in just the same way as the emblems, carvings, statues and writing were. In fact, when one considers the context in which these symbolisms are found, it is not surprising to see the same ideas being applied to the same pharaonic funerary architecture, albeit through a different artistic medium.

Whether or not there is one specific meaning central to the circular symbolism at first glance seems difficult to say, and as with so much Egyptian ideology, the symbolism is often multi-layered and complex, and different ideas were often hybridized into new and changing forms. The Old Kingdom was an extremely innovative period and despite the fact that many of the pharaonic traditions had much older origins, the way in which they were incorporated into the new funerary monuments was frequently novel. Nevertheless, the idea of a protective circle-based perimeter surrounding the pharaonic tomb chamber, and surrounding the whole pharaonic tomb itself, for eternity, is something that clearly fits with the cultural context from which the symbolism arose, with its particular cosmology, iconography, technology and ideology.

There was also a celestial, heavenly, aspect associated with the shen circle symbolism, beyond just the abstract representations of the concepts of protection and eternity, and in this context it is notable that Khufu's pyramid was called the 'Horizon of Khufu'. The horizon in Egyptian cosmology was thought of as the boundary between the earth and the sky. Likewise, tomb chambers were not just seen as protective strongholds, but were also seen as miniature versions of the Egyptian world, with stars and stellar sky scenes painted on the ceilings, while earthly themes of daily life were often painted on the walls.

Figure 43 God Heh from Entrance to Ramesses II's jubilee temple

According to Egyptologist J.P. Allen, the word on which shen is based, Snw, 'circle' refers to the circle of the world, and the combination of the Snw with the king's name inside it originally indicated that the king has

Chapter 3. The Symbolism

dominion over the whole world (Allen 2001: 65). In Middle Kingdom and New Kingdom inscriptions, the cartouche or shen ring reflects the phrase 'all that the sun disk circles (shen)' (Quirke 2001: 123).

During the course of this study, R. Wilkinson's excellent book "reading Egyptian art" provided the most helpful information regarding the shen. In his book he devotes two pages each to several dozen symbols commonly found in Egyptian artworks. Short excerpts from the excellent content from his book are quoted below: (Wilkinson 2003: 192 & 193):

Figure 44 Horus holding Shen

Shen (hieroglyphic sign V9)

"Being without beginning or end, the circle evokes the concept of eternity through its form, and its solar aspect is symbolised by the sun disk often depicted in the centre of the *shen* sign. These ideas were probably the origin of this hieroglyph which is found in words connected with the verbal root *shenu* meaning "encircle," and which in its later elongated form became the cartouche which surrounded the Egyptian king's birth and throne names. Perhaps from this particular context the *shen* sign also took on the connotation of protection – as the device which excluded all inimical elements from the royal name. The *shen* may appear with both of these meanings – "eternity" and "protection" – in Egyptian art. As a sign in the former, the hieroglyph is frequently associated with representations of Heh, the god of eternity, and often forms the base of the notched palm-branch, symbolising "years," which is held by this deity [Figure 43]......The sign is perhaps most commonly associated with the avian form of the falcon god Horus and the various vulture goddesses, however. These divine birds are frequently depicted holding the *shen* in their claws, hovering above the king and guarding him beneath their outstretched wings. The *shen* signs proffered by these avian deities may be regarded as symbols of eternity, and therefore life, but it is possible that the signs also carry the connotation of protection, and this double significance would certainly seem to be present in many of the small decorative items and amulets which use the sign in their design."

Cartouche (hieroglyphic sign V10):

"The term "cartouche" is a relatively modern one, which was bestowed on this hieroglyph by the soldiers of Napoleon's expedition to Egypt, who saw in the sign the likeness of the cartridges or "cartouches" used in their own guns. The Egyptian name for the cartouche like that of the *shen* sign – was derived from the verb *sheni*: "to encircle," and the earliest forms of the cartouche in which the king's name was written were in fact circular and identical with that sign. Early in Egyptian history, however, the form of the *shen* ring was lengthened in order to hold the increased number of hieroglyphs resulting from longer royal names and fuller orthography. In this way the *shen* continued to be used as a sign with its own meanings while the cartouche became the standard holder of the royal name.....While one of the connotations of the cartouche seems to have related to solar symbolism (since the device may have originally represented that which was encircled by the sun – the realm of the king), an apotropaic [to ward off evil] function relating to the protection of the king's name was also extremely important. This protective function may be alluded to in the design of cartouche shaped royal sarcophagi from the Eighteenth Dynasty on. Certainly, it would seem fitting to place the deceased king within a chest signifying his name and person, but the sense that protective imagery is involved is heightened by the inscriptions and representations that were also added to many sarcophagi. In the tomb of Thutmose III, in the Valley of the Kings, the entire burial chamber – as well as the sarcophagus – was constructed in the shape of the cartouche."

The use of the symbol of the shen/cartouche as a design element in the sarcophagus [Figure 45] and the tomb chamber itself is a key example of how artistic iconography and physical architecture can become intertwined. The cases described above also show how the symbolism of the shen was certainly considered an aspect associated with royal funerary architecture, and more specifically, with the form of the chambers and the sarcophagi.

One of the clearest examples demonstrating the link between the royal tomb, the royal sarcophagus, the cartouches and the shens is found in the tomb of the pharaoh Tuthmosis III, and this is worth describing in some detail at this stage. This tomb, designated KV 34, is the royal burial tomb of the pharaoh Thuthmosis III, and is found in the Valley of the Kings west of modern day Luxor, ancient Waset. It contains the earliest example of 'the Amduat', a funerary text and artwork, in this case drafted out on the walls in the 18th dynasty (c.a. 1425 B.C.), but thought to be based on an older tradition and older texts.

Chapter 3. The Symbolism

The tomb was one the earliest to be built in the Valley of the Kings, and it is located high on a cliff face, at the top of one of the wadis furthest from the entrance to the main valley. The tomb has several chambers, and the passages together form an unusual dog-leg shape, with a trapezoidal antechamber, followed further inside by the cartouche shaped royal burial chamber. The sarcophagus of the pharaoh remains largely intact in this chamber despite damage from robbers who entered the tomb in antiquity. The sarcophagus is also roughly cartouche shaped, but equally of relevance are the goddesses Isis and Nephthys shown at the end of the sarcophagus protecting the head and feet of the pharaoh. The pair are shown kneeling and holding shen rings. After being ransacked in antiquity, the tomb then lay undiscovered again until 1898 when it was excavated by Victor Loret (1859-1946), the head of the Egyptian Antiquities Service at the time. As for the mummy of Tuthmosis III himself, this was removed and rewrapped during Dynasty 21, and was found in its original outer coffin in the 'Deir el-Bahri cache', TT 320, in 1881. Two damaged mummies found in KV 34 were also disturbed, indicating that the tomb was entered again after their burial.

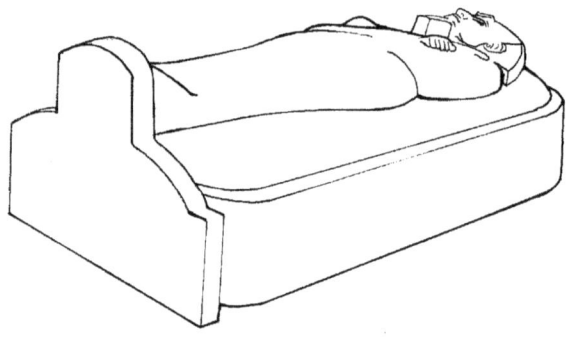

Figure 45 Cartouche shaped sarcophagus of Merneptah from KV8

On the walls of the burial chamber were found the earliest examples of the written verses and graphical arrangements of the Amduat liturgy. The Amduat, or Imydwat, is also known as 'the book of what is in the netherworld'. In this case the artwork and writing is in an unusual, naïve style, with stick like figures drawn on a yellow background, thought to deliberately resemble ink writing onto aged papyrus.

It is a series of murals that portray the voyage and rebirth of the sun through the hours of the night, and relates this to the rebirth of the Pharaoh after his death. The Amduat is a description of the journey of the sun god through the nightworld; a world that is also the world of the deceased. Although it is a funerary text of the New Kingdom it is thought that its origins lie in the much older Pyramid Texts of the Old Kingdom (first seen in the pyramid of Unas at Saqqara c.a. 2345 B.C.), which also describe the journey of the pharaoh towards the afterlife and the netherworld. At the start of the Amduat, the names of many gods and goddesses are listed so that the pharaoh will recognise them as he travels through the 12 hours of the night, which are represented individually on the panels of the mural. These gods and goddesses can either aid the pharaoh, or must be defeated by the pharaoh with the aid of the others.

A photograph of part of the Amduat from Tuthmosis III's tomb is shown below [Figure 46]. It shows the events of 'the 5th hour' from the east wall of the tomb, which is the most relevant to this work.

Figure 46 The symbolic tomb of Osiris from the 5th hour of the Amduat in KV34

The fifth hour of the Amduat represents the transformation of the pharaoh's spirit within 'the secret cave of Osiris' (Osiris being the funerary god). The transformation takes place underneath a pyramid shaped mound, and demonstrates the ability of the pharaoh's soul to transform after death, and ascend to the heavens.

The most interesting aspect of the fifth hour of the Amduat, for our immediate purposes, is the form of this 'secret cave of Osiris'. In this scene the cave or tomb of Osiris is shown as an oval enclosure, deep under the pyramid-shaped hill. Right at the top of this mound sit Isis and Nephthys in the form of two kites (Egyptian birds of prey). As mentioned above, these two goddesses are also often found protecting the head and feet of sarcophagi, as they do on the sarcophagus in this tomb chamber of KV34, and for example on the ends of sarcophagi belonging to the pharaohs Amenhotep II (Wilkinson 1999: 85), Tuthmosis I and Hateshepsut. The oval cave or chamber of Osiris portrayed on the mural is effectively also cartouche shaped, and within the enclosed oval space is found the god Sokar. Sokar was the patron god of the whole necropolis of Memphis, which included Giza and Saqqara from the earliest times, and it is thought that the name Saqqara is in fact derived from his name. Sokar, with his falcon's head and pair of wings, seems to have symbolised the spiritual nature of the soul of the pharaoh, and its ability to escape the body of the deceased and to ascend to the paradise in the heavens. This rebirth of the pharaoh's soul after death is the crucial ideology represented by the whole funerary

Chapter 3. The Symbolism

liturgy, and so Sokar was absolutely central to the ritual belief system that underpinned the pharaonic religion and the Egyptian culture as a whole. This cave or chamber has also been referred to as the cavern of Sokar (Hornung 1999: 37).

The common protective themes repeated in the oval iconography of the tomb of Osiris and/or Sokar are echoed in the form of the pharaonic tomb of Tuthmosis III itself, and by the form his sarcophagus.

As far as this thesis is concerned, however, the most relevant aspects are the association of the forms of the cartouche and the shen with both the pharaonic tomb and the sarcophagus itself. In this case in KV34 the shen is seen at the head and feet of the cartouche shaped sarcophagus, while the tomb itself is actually oval and cartouche shaped. The walls of the tomb display a liturgy portraying the transformation and resurrection of the spiritual nature of the pharaoh in the form of Sokar, and again this takes place within an oval or cartouche shaped enclosure, related to the funerary god Osiris. On other pharaonic sarcophagi, such as on that of Nectanebo II now in the British Museum (c.a. 345 B.C.), extracts from the Amduat are actually inscribed on the sarcophagus itself, so that the close relationship between sarcophagus and tomb is again demonstrated. The recently restored granite sarcophagus of Ramesses III at the Fitzwilliam Museum in Cambridge, England, is another fine example of a cartouche shaped sarcophagus.

Figure 47 Isis from the sarcophagus of Queen Hatshepsut, recut for Tuthmosis I

The shen and cartouche represented eternity, protection and encirclement. These ideas dovetail well with the deliberate incorporation of encircling and protecting symbolism into the architecture of the tombs of the pharaohs.

The figure of Isis holding the shen ring shown above [Figure 47] is taken from the design on the end of the sarcophagus of Hateshepsut, recut for her father Tuthmosis I. Like the other sarcophagi from the Valley of the Kings discussed above it dates to the 18th dynasty of the New Kingdom, and in this case from the reign of Hatshepsut, c.a. 1460 B.C. It is made of painted quartzite and is now on view in the Museum of Fine Arts, Boston (Accession number 04.278.1). The sarcophagus was taken from KV20 in the Valley of the Kings, Thebes, in 1903-4, after being discovered by Howard Carter of the Egyptian Antiquities Service The figure of the goddess Isis (wife of Osiris and also known as 'queen of the throne') shown above is taken from the lower, feet end, of the sarcophagus, while Nephthys strikes a similar pose at the upper, head end of the sarcophagus, again holding a shen ring. While these goddesses are found at these locations on sarcophagi for many hundreds of years following the innovative 18th dynasty, they are most often shown with the shen in the earlier period. In later times the two goddesses are often shown in the same locations, but with outstretched, raised, arms, or with protective wings spread out wide with their arms, but with no shen rings.

Part of the reason for this change may have been the difficult demands of artistic construction. If we consider the difficulty the artist above had in successfully portraying Isis holding the shen from the side, as a result of the strict cannons or rules of Egyptian art, this resulted in her being shown with only one arm. It seems possible that artistic licence was the reason that this shen pose was abandoned in favour of a more easily drawn spread armed pose. Nevertheless, in the early examples the goddesses and the shen are clearly associated with the protection of the head and feet of the sarcophagus.

Figure 48 Lady Shepenhor with the shen rings protecting head

Another good example of the shen in its role as protector of the deceased is from the tomb of Khabekhnet, from the time of Ramesses II (c.a. 1250 B.C.), and is from the tomb mural rather than the sides or ends of a sarcophagus. This is the mummification scene shown on the north wall of the tomb of the artisan, TT2, in the

Chapter 3. The Symbolism

cemetery of the workmen's village of Deir el-Medina at Thebes. This is not a royal scene, but Isis and Nephthys are nevertheless shown attending the head and feet of the mummified deceased, on their knees again, holding large shen rings at either end of the body.

Another later example of the use of the Shen ring as a protective funerary emblem is on the mummy of the lady Shepenhor, now displayed in the collection of the Hunterian Museum at the University of Glasgow [Figure 48]. This was discovered in Thebes and dates to c.a. 600 B.C., during the 26th Dynasty. It is spectacularly coloured with vivid reds, greens, blues and yellows, and whereas the shen is usually held at the top of the head by Nephthys, in this case the rings are shown held at the sides of the head, by claws representing the feet of Horus. This protective bird theme is reinforced by the ring of protective feathers around the crown of the mummy, as though protective wings were being held about its head. This recalls the earliest representations showing Horus carrying the shen above the pharaoh's head.

On the beautifully decorated cartonnage sarcophagus of Djed-Khonsou-iou-ef-ankh [
Figure *49*], from the 21-22nd dynasties, c.a. 1061-715 B.C., now in the Louvre, we can see another use of the shen symbol, this time in conjunction with the symbol of rebirth, the scarab beetle Kheper. Kheper is often shown raising the sun disc above his head, symbolising the rebirth of the sun every day, and the concept of rebirth itself. In this case the beetle also lifts up the shen with his feet, so that we see the symbols of protection and eternity being linked with the symbols of rebirth and the sun. By comparing and contrasting these various representations together, we can start to build up a fuller understanding of the meanings carried by the symbols in the minds of the Egyptians.

Possibly the finest example of the use of the shen symbol from the Giza plateau, and from the pyramid age itself, is that held in the hand of the goddess Hathor in one of the finest pieces of sculpture ever to have emerged from antiquity. The representation of Hathor is part of one of the famous 'Triads of King Menkaure' that were uncovered in 1910 by George Reisner during his excavation of the Valley temples. The photograph below is of the triad statue in the Egyptian Museum, Cairo (JE 46499). It is carved from solid schist, is almost a metre in height, and immortalised the pharaoh and his two goddesses in realistic form [Figure 50].

This masterpiece of royal sculpture from the Old Kingdom clearly shows the substantial anatomical knowledge of the artist, and an ability to produce well-proportioned statues in polished hard stone with complete perfection. The effective proportioning of the lithe bodies of the king and his goddesses may show some connection to the increased use of standardised measurement, as this allowed a much more precise and systematic approach to be taken to producing lifelike statues. Many hundreds of years later, when the Greeks learnt the skills of proportional sculpture, they commented on the importance of the careful measurement that allowed the construction of realistic anthropometric statues.

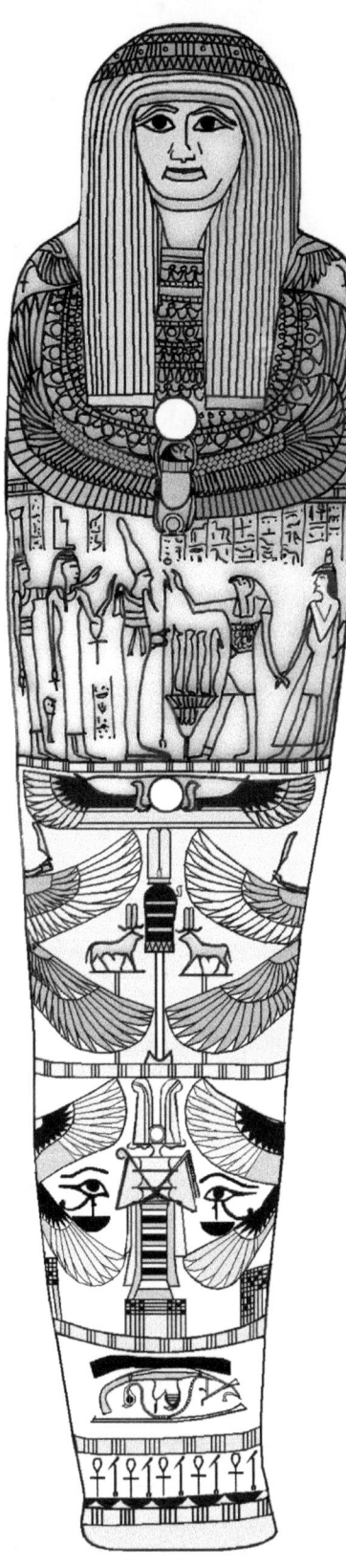

Figure 49 Cartonnage of Djed-Khonsou-iou-ef-ankh

Chapter 3. The symbolism

Figure 50 Last of the great pyramid builders

Chapter 3. The symbolism

During the Old Kingdom, measurement may first have become widely used in the arts and crafts due to its widespread use in the great monumental construction projects that had taken place in the 100 years leading up to Menkaure's rule, when this magnificent statue was produced.

The high standards of craft technology demonstrated by these triads clearly show that a substantial increase in capabilities had been achieved since the time of Saqqara, and this is something that is seen in almost every aspect of Egyptian culture through the 3rd and 4th dynasties. In this representation the king wears the white Hedjet crown of Upper Egypt. On his left side is the personification of a goddess of the 17th nome district of Upper Egypt. It is thought that these statues including nome gods were associated with ceremonies whereby the rulers of each nome region undertook to protect the pharaoh during his reign.

Hathor, with the Shen ring in hand, standing on the pharaoh's right hand side, reinforces this message of protection. One can certainly envisage the handsome trio gazing out over the great works that their ancestors had created on the Giza Plateau.

The protective perimeter represented by the shen delineated a sacred space around the pharaoh's resting place just as the cartouche perimeter around his name protected the pharaoh in life.

Finally, it is quite poignant to conclude with the observation that one of the very few original inscriptions recovered from the body of the pyramid of Khufu [Figure 51] was the pharaoh's name sketched in the rough hand of a builder or mason. This cartouche was a hand written note of the intended destination of the stone after quarrying and shaping, and it has survived only because of its well-protected location in the relieving spaces above the King's burial chamber. In this case, the physical building around the inscription has protected the cartouche, and both together have succeeded in preserving the pharaoh's name for us to see today.

Figure 51 Cartouche of pharaoh Khufu from the Great Pyramid

The association of the shen rings with the sun and the perimeters of the sky extended the ideology of eternal protection from the sarcophagus, to the pharaonic tomb chamber, and eventually on to the protection of the tomb building and pyramid superstructure as a whole. The associated concepts of the 'limits of the sky' took this symbolism a stage further, to extend the protective symbolism across the Egyptian territory, and right to the horizons of the Egyptian universe as a whole.

This multi-scaled ideology was incorporated into the pharaonic tomb architecture through the use of circular numbers and proportions that expressed these circular concepts symbolically in rectilinear stone.

This circular symbolism in rectilinear architecture can be seen as an important symbolic belief system that helped support and ensure the longevity and stability of pharaonic rule, in life and beyond.

From the perspective of the Ancient Egyptians, geometry and arithmetic empowered them to organise massive monumental building projects that physically protected the pharaoh for eternity. In many ways, the geometry, the symbolism and the enduring limestone and granite reality display various aspects of one brilliant pharaonic civilisation.

Chapter 4. Methodology, analysis and discussion of mathematics

4. Methodology, analysis and discussion of mathematics

"the ancient Egyptians' constructions are the best evidence of their mathematical capabilities"
Professor Miroslav Verner.

This chapter outlines the methodology used to analyse the architectural features and the associated mathematical data. In it, I explain the principles that were applied in the analysis, and then expand on the Ancient Egyptian mathematical context that can be developed as a result.

The analysis of the data presented in this book took place over several years, and several ground rules were established along the way to ensure that the correct conclusions were ultimately reached.

The four principal ground rules were as follows:

- The scientific method and logical argument must be applied throughout
- The data must be interpreted within its cultural context, meaning through an analysis strictly based on cubits, unit fractions and sekeds
- All direct and circumstantial evidence from both textual and archaeological source materials have to be included in the new explanation, rather than including just a partial body of data as has been the case previously
- Proper engineering judgement must be applied during the analysis, through the use of suitable tolerances and a proper evaluation of the precision and accuracy of ancient construction and modern surveys alike

The first point means that a strict methodology was used to analyse and reach conclusions from the evidence, facts and the data set as a whole. This was carried out as many, if not most, of the publications surrounding this subject have assumption and premises in their arguments that are clearly incorrect, or which are not applied consistently or logically. To correctly interpret the facts, the scientific method and logical argument must be applied strictly throughout, and instead of trying to derive a single universal theory from the data, an understanding of the real situation must rather be shaped by the evidence and facts, and not vice versa. The most widely known example of circular symbolism being applied in the architecture is in the primary dimensions of the Great Pyramid, but to follow correct methodology we cannot reach any conclusion from this one single case. To be sure that this was expressed on purpose, and not by chance, it was necessary to examine the other buildings and the wider cultural context, and to identify any other examples of the same. Once that had been done, a historical developmental process had to be established into which this tradition clearly fit. The process through which the pyramids developed from the earlier 'mastaba' tombs is already well established, so that the circular symbolism had to be understood within that established cultural context.

Secondly, in chapter two, examples were laid out that show the gradual and developing technical application of the symbolism with regards to a historical developmental sequence, and through six mutually supporting examples. This sequence, which was part of the process whereby the mastabas evolved into the 'step' and then 'true' pyramids, means that the condition for an established sequence has been satisfied (Edwards 1979: 33; Emery 1991: 119; Lehner 1997: 80). In the previous chapter the meaning of the symbolism was interpreted within its cultural context, so that this satisfied the requirement for a continuous developmental sequence that fits within the cultural context of Old Kingdom Egypt.

Rather than a universal rule, the cultural evidence in Egypt in fact points to continuous development and change, and rather than each pyramid demonstrating the same characteristics, they are in fact all different, so that the general impression emerging is that each one was personified or tailored for each pharaoh, as well as being an expression of the latest methods that had been developed. Traditions developed and rules were made and adhered to, but they were also broken and changed if necessary or when desirable.

Thirdly, we must be scrupulously faithful to all the circumstantial evidence from other sources, including textual, so that we are understanding the data with regards to its own cultural context as far as is possible. All of the evidence must be considered, as opposed to cherry picking data that fits a preconceived conclusion, or ignoring evidence that is inconvenient, or simply labelling it as anomalous data. Instead of projecting our own systems of thought into a culture in which they don't belong, we must allow the data to dictate to us exactly how it should be understood. In this regard we must literally learn to 'think like an Egyptian' to understand what Egyptians did. As has been mentioned already, one good simple approach in this respect is that instead of using metres, and degrees and decimals, we must force ourselves to use and think in cubits, sekeds and unit fractions when considering the architectural evidence. Only once this transformation has been completed can we understand all of the data, and therefore develop the ability to synthesise it into one historical narrative. This process is nevertheless an ongoing one, and this monograph is intended to ensure that further discussion and consideration of all of the related evidence continues.

Fourthly, we must analyse the facts from a scientific and engineering basis that correctly appreciates the subtleties and realities of construction processes and materials, erosion and measurement tolerances, and the importance of 'significant figures' when quoting and understanding measurement data. Too many publications have become

Chapter 4. Methodology, analysis and discussion of mathematics

overwhelmed by unrealistically quoting figures to excessive numbers of significant figures, or conversely, quoting figures with such a low accuracy and with no variation tolerances so that their actual meaning cannot be evaluated. Quoting figures with dozens of zeros confuses the issue, and claims to excessive amounts of accuracy can be made where none was ever intended. Conversely, quoting a figure rounded to the nearest metre, or tens of metres, can render an understanding of the actual levels of construction precision impossible, if the construction accuracy exceeded the accuracy to which measurements of the structures are quoted in publications.

Too many existing publications have accepted similar premises, yet have failed to apply them consistently and therefore derive incorrect conclusions from the facts.

After a strict analysis of the individual cases, facts, and the data set as a whole, in strict accordance with the four methodological rules above, several issues slowly became apparent.

With respect to logical conclusions that can be derived from the data, firstly, the ancient Egyptians did not have a full understanding of a stand-alone 'ratio', with the symbol pi that we are familiar with today.

Secondly, the evidence strongly suggests that they were nevertheless able to translate the proportions of a circle into rectilinear ratios, and not only that, they were able to use the relevant numerical values, expressed in cubits, that present themselves most readily from the natural proportions of a circle. We now all now 'know' that 22/7 is the ratio of a circle's circumference to its diameter, but for the Ancient Egyptians a fraction of this type was impossible to even write down, as their system was a 'unit fraction' system.

Therefore, when they did use this number 22/7, it would have been written as $3 + 1/7^{th}$, and not as 22/7, and was not understood as a stand-alone ratio, but only as the circumference length of a circle of 1 cubit across. Whilst this is not modern pi as it is known today, it most certainly is an early precursor version of pi, and is the first known use of the numbers 22 and 7 in relation to the proportions of a circle in history. That in itself is a substantial conclusion to draw regarding the achievements of the Egyptian scribes, and their contribution to the development and history of mathematics and geometry.

In order to demonstrate that this number would have been obtainable, Egyptologist John Legon showed how the 3+1/7th circumference value could have been established by using very direct practical methods, such as drawing a large circle with a diameter of 1 cubit onto a flat surface, and then measuring the circumference with a length of cord that is equal to the diameter (Legon 1979). After laying the measuring cord around the circumference three times, the remaining length is very precisely one seventh of the total length of the diameter. This remainder is a simple subdivision of the cubit and it is this 'coincidence' that means that this would be a procedure that would have been well within the capabilities of the Old Kingdom Egyptians. Therefore, it is relatively straightforward to discover that the circumference of a circle is $3+1/7^{th}$ times its diameter, and quite logical to see that this is in fact precisely what the Ancient Egyptians did.

It is very probable that this simple procedure relating to a circle provided the origins for the unusually subdivided 7 palm cubit rules. The very earliest attestations of the use of the cubit in Egypt are of the cubit of 7 parts, such as is seen at Saqqara, and there is no alternative explanation for this that seems more plausible.

As has been discussed, this 7 palm cubit would have had the additional quality that the diagonal of this measure, when setting out in a cubit square, was very close to 10 palms, this being 98.99% accurate. These two basic fundamental geometrical properties of a 7 part rule, the circular and the diagonal numerical values that it produces, seem to be the features that appealed to the Old Kingdom architects, agricultural land surveyors, tomb artists and sculptors who first devised and applied a standardised measurement system. The basis of the choice of 7 parts is practical, for agricultural and constructional measurement reasons, and the accuracy of the systems is approximate but good.

It is exactly this sort of functional and practical mensuration system that we expect to see in the Old Kingdom cultural context, and all of the facts and data confirms this directly. It is entirely reasonable that this was the case.

A further increase in the complexity of the basic mathematical and geometric systems stemmed from this basic starting point through the 3rd and 4th dynasties, and is also observable in the architecture. This, again, is exactly what one would expect to see as their technical abilities grew through practice and application in accordance with the developing tomb architecture and the developing society as a whole.

In the early case of Saqqara, for example, the great temenos wall is extremely close to $3+1/7^{th}$ times the 1000 cubits of the temenos north-south centreline length that Lauer found to have been an important architectural feature. This is a relatively straightforward expression of the circular proportions.

In the later case of Meidum, Petrie found that the circular symbolism was expressed in the principal dimensions of the pyramid structure itself, including in its perimeter, rather than in the perimeter of the temenos wall, which was relegated in importance to a secondary role at Meidum and in pyramids built thereafter. In addition to the actual proportions of the building at Meidum, Petrie found that the numerical values of the dimensions of the

Chapter 4. Methodology, analysis and discussion of mathematics

structure in royal cubits pointed to 44 and 7 having been the relevant numbers applied. In this case it is the ratio of a circle's radius, and not diameter, to its circumference that is expressed in this structure's proportions.

There is no suggestion here of uncovering a master theory, we are simply interpreting the architectural symbolism as it was used and the various ways in which the symbolism was applied, directly from the architecture [Figure 52].

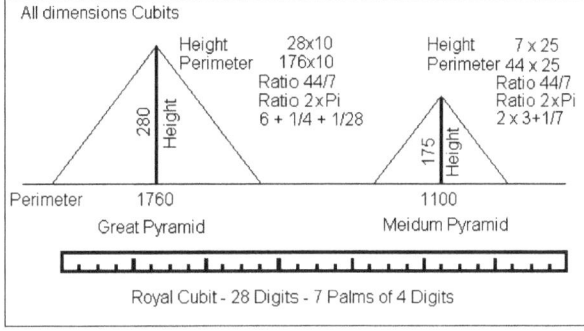

Figure 52 Comparison of data from Khufu and Meidum pyramids

From the pyramid tombs at Giza we can see that by the time they were built a new, related, but more complex set of numbers were being expressed in the primary dimensions (as opposed to the proportions which are the same circular proportions), apparently related to 28 rather than 7, and in the Great Pyramid's case, with a perimeter of 1760 cubits.

These numbers at first sight seems less directly linked to the circle's natural numerical approximations.

It is only if we consider that the proportions exhibited at Meidum and the Great Pyramid were based on the radius to circumference proportion, and not the simpler diameter to circumference proportion as seen at Saqqara, that a plausible reason for the jump to 28 as a relevant number, from 7, 44, and $3+1/7^{th}$, becomes apparent.

The explanation is that when the Egyptian unit fraction $3+1/7^{th}$ is doubled arithmetically, as would be required when moving from calculating a circumference from a diameter to calculating a circumference from a radius, the fraction yielded is $6+2/7^{th}$. In Egyptian unit fractions, however, the 2/7ths cannot be written down, and the whole fraction must be expressed as $6 + 1/4^{th} + 1/28^{th}$ [Figure 53].

This equation is shown below in a form similar to how it could have been written down at the time, and by way of this reconstruction it becomes clear that the cubit rule is in fact well fitted for both radius to circumference, and diameter to circumference, calculations, by way of being divisible into 7^{ths}, as well as 28ths, and 1/4s.

As has been discussed previously, the cubit and its subdivisions developed alongside the parallel geometric developments, and within the restrictions imposed by the unit fraction system, so that the numbers fit the practical functions.

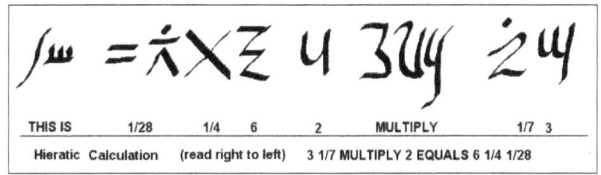

Figure 53 what the developing calculation could have looked like in hieratic

The above discussion remains faithful to the cultural context, with unit fractions, with the 7 and 28 part royal cubits of the correct dimensions, with the actual proportions and numerical dimensions of the Old Kingdom structures, and with the developmental sequence matching the known cultural history. It also remains faithful to seked gradients, but this will be discussed later with reference to other publications that discuss sekeds.

This equation, drawn out through the strict application of the methodology and the logical arguments, may help us to understand the development of the geometry that took place in conjunction with the tomb architecture. It certainly helps us understand why the 28 digit cubit can be directly compared to the 280 cubit height of the great pyramid [Figure 52]. Thus was because both developed together, and both were based on the proportions of the circle.

In the comparison table at the end of the data chapter [Figure 36], the proportions listed in the final column are presented as being either once or twice the circular ratio. The change in the chronological sequence seen in the proportions after Saqqara, from once to twice, also parallels the numerical changes from 7 to 28 observed in the applied numbers, when the architectural dimensions are considered in cubits. This supports an interpretation whereby the architects started to express the radius to circumference proportions, as well as the older and simpler diameter to circumference ratio.

The rise in complexity seen through the Old Kingdom encompassed several skills that developed simultaneously, were inter-dependant and were intimately related. These included mathematics, mensuration, stone cutting and construction technology and geometry. By tracking their simultaneous development through the strict application of archaeological methodology, we can confirm that the earliest geometric methods evidenced anywhere in history were created in conjunction with the pyramids of Old Kingdom Egypt.

This concludes the first half of this monograph on Old Kingdom royal funerary architecture. So far it has

Chapter 4. Methodology, analysis and discussion of mathematics

focussed on the cultural context of Ancient Egypt, the raw data from the archaeological evidence, and developed and applied a new set of four methodological ground rules to the evidence to draw out further meaning.

In addition, the traditional culture belief system of the Egyptians has been explored, and the probable conceptual meaning underlying the symbolism applied in the architecture has been identified.

The chapters that now follow in the second half of the monograph are intended to provide background information that supports this interpretation from some of the foremost authorities on the architecture of ancient Egypt. It also has the objective of tackling every substantive argument that has used against this interpretation in the past, and to show where these arguments were incorrect.

Chapter 5.   Arguments from authorities

5. Arguments from authorities

"... A new stir arose when one day I brought back from Smith's bookstall, in 1866, a volume by Piazzi Smyth, Our Inheritance in the Great Pyramid. The views, in conjunction with his old friendship for the author, strongly attracted my father, and for some years I was urged on in what seemed so enticing a field of coincidence. I little thought how, fifteen years later, I should reach the "ugly little fact which killed the beautiful theory"; but it was this interest which led my father to encourage me to go out and do the survey of the Great Pyramid"

(Petrie 1931: 13)

This chapter briefly summarises quotes from some of the top Egyptologists and historical mathematicians of the 20th century. All the authors effectively state in writing that the circular symbolism observed in the funerary architecture was deliberately expressed there. Nevertheless, none provide a convincing explanation for why this was done. The chapter also lists equivalent conclusions reached by experts from associated fields who have also stated their position on this subject matter in writing.

Whilst 'argument from authority' alone is certainly not enough to demonstrate the reality of any proposal, it can strengthen the case for the proposal when considered in conjunction with the facts. This combined approach can certainly facilitate people's acceptance of those facts, and so quotes from some of the major authorities on Ancient Egyptian architecture are listed below.

The conclusions of these Egyptologists quoted below, in conjunction with the data already observed in the architectural and textual evidence, allows us to accept that the use of these circular proportions in the designs was not just a question of chance occurrence, or the by-product of a certain method, but was a logical, and to some extents systematic application of circular symbolism in the primary dimensions of the pharaonic funerary architecture. It was not, however, a universal architectural rule that we should expect to see applied in every case, and the grey area between what constitutes traditional circular symbolism and what constitutes a mathematical understanding of 'pi' is also something that will have to be clarified.

Here are some quotes then from experts who were largely correct in their interpretations of the data, and who successfully remained faithful to the facts and evidence:

Most recently, Egyptologist Dr Bojana Mojsov, in her recent book about the Egyptian funerary god "Osiris", wrote about pyramids and Old Kingdom architecture saying: (2005: 26): *"The architects seem have been aware of the mathematical properties now represented by the letter "Pi". Possibly obtained from practical experience, this knowledge had a profound influence on their ability to design and build complex structures. Monumentality, elegance of line, and minimal decoration were among the glories of this age"* (Mojsov 2005).

Egyptologist Professor Miroslav Verner, author of 'The Pyramids, their Archaeology and History" wrote: *"...the ancient Egyptians' constructions are the best evidence of their mathematical capabilities. Let us take for instance, the Great Pyramid in Giza. If we imagine a circle whose radius is the height of the pyramid, then the circumference is identical with the base of the pyramid. This could be achieved only if the wall had the correct angle, and everything had to be calculated in advance. We can conclude that although the ancient Egyptians may have never precisely defined the value of pi, in practice they used it."* (Verner 2001: 70).

As already referred to, Flinders Petrie, author of 'The Pyramids and Temples of Gizeh", the first accurate surveyor of Giza and the excavator and surveyor of the Pyramid of Meidum, also concluded, after many years in the field in Egypt: *"but these relations of areas and of circular ratio are so systematic that we should grant that they were in the builders design"* (Petrie 1940: 30).

Earlier in the chapter quoted above, he wrote more specifically, that: *"We conclude therefore that the approximation of 7 to 22 as the ratio of diameter to circumference was recognised"* (Petrie 1940: 27).

Surprisingly, Petrie never suggested a plausible reason for why these circular proportion should have been included in the designs. Perhaps if he had been aware of the supporting data from Saqqara he would have arrived at the correct meaning.

From outside the field of Egyptology, Archaeo-astronomer S.C. Haack, author of a paper entitled "A practical explanation for the dimensions of the Egyptian pyramids", from the 1976 Proceedings of the Nebraska Academy of Sciences wrote: *"This is consistent with the architecture of all the pyramids built during the fourth dynasty in that most of their angles can be expressed in terms of ratios of small integers or an integer and Pi"*

BBC television producer and writer Paul Jordan wrote a section in G.G. Fagan's book *'Archaeological Fantasies: How Pseudoarchaeology Misrepresents the Past and Misleads the Public'* (Jordan 2006: 120). Although his chapter on Ancient Egypt has the objective of rejecting claims for the Egyptians to be credited for their achievements, he does correctly summarise Petrie's position regarding the circular symbolism: *"An engineer called William Petrie* [Petrie's Father] *got caught up in Smyth's speculations and longed to measure the Great Pyramid with even better instruments. His son William Flinders Petrie was keen to find out if it all really stood*

Chapter 5.   Arguments from authorities

up by determining the still partly-obscured basal dimensions of the monument and measuring not just one pyramid but its companions and indeed the whole surrounding topography. Flinders Petrie satisfied himself as to the claimed extreme accuracy of the Great Pyramid's layout, but he also noticed those signs of slightly botched execution and unfinished-ness that always dog the Egyptian monuments (like all things human). He accepted that there were ancient units of measure to be discerned in the sacred structure, but not the sacred cubit in place of the traditional royal cubit of around 21 inches. His base measurements did not match Smyth's, partly because he differed as to what to measure**, and although he thought** pi *was there* [my emphasis]*, he could not see the days of the year* [Smyth theorised that the edge of the pyramid was 365 cubits in length, reflecting accurate knowledge of the number days in a year] *His* Pyramids and Temples of Gizeh *(Petrie 1883) found him wryly amused to realise that when he had started his work fifteen years before he could little know it would be himself who "would reach the ugly little fact which killed the beautiful theory".* The theory that Petrie 'killed' referred to here was Smyth's 365 cubit theory.

Next, a Dr H.C. Schepler wrote a series of articles entitled "The Chronology of Pi" in Mathematics Magazine in 1950 concerning the mathematical historical development of approximations for the ratio of pi. He listed at the very start of the article: *"3000 B.C. The Pyramids (Egypt). 3 1/7 (3.142857......). The sides and heights of the pyramids of Cheops and of Sneferu at Gizeh are in the ratio 11:7, which makes the ratio of half the perimeter to the height 3 1/7. In 1853 H. C. Agnew, Esq., London, published a letter from Alexandria on evidence of this ratio found in the pyramids being connected or related to the problem of the quadrature of the circle."*(The letter was originally written in 1838) (Schepler 1950).

Beatrice Lumpkin, Associate Professor of Mathematics, Chicago City Colleges, retired, wrote in 1997: *"Either way it is taken, it is clear that the Egyptian value for pi was more accurate than any other approximation of ancient times. I would suggest that we have too few mathematical documents at this time to reject, out of hand, the possibility that the ratio of the Great Pyramid semiperimeter to its heights was significant."*(Quoted in Hollenback 1997).

Most concisely, and almost entirely correctly, Egyptologists Somers Clarke and R. Englebach (who were referred to in chapter 3) wrote in their book: '*Ancient Egyptian Construction and Architecture*' that: *"The pyramid seems to be a sun-emblem, and in those of Sneferu at Meydûm and Khufu at Gîza the proportions are such that, if a circle be imagined whose circumference is equal to the perimeter of the base of the pyramid, the radius of that circle will be its height. This gives an angle of 51°51' for the angle of the casing"* (Clarke and Engelbach 1991: 118).

Most importantly, Professor I.E.S Edwards, author of '*The Pyramids of Egypt*' and of whom Dr Mark Lehner, author of '*The Complete Pyramids*', referred to as 'the great pyramid authority', (Lehner 1997: 34) wrote: *"The normal angle of incline was about 52° - a slope which, in the Pyramid of Meidum and in the Great Pyramid, would have resulted if the height had been made to correspond with the radius of a circle the circumference of which was equal to the perimeter of the Pyramid at ground level. The northern stone Pyramid at Dashur, with its gradient of 43°35', provides the only striking exception to this rule"* (Edwards 1979: 269).

By 1931, when Petrie was writing his autobiography, he had stopped replying to those who still could not accept the simple fact that the Great Pyramid and the Meidum Pyramid had been deliberately designed by the Old Kingdom pyramid builders to have the same height to perimeter ratio as a circle's radius has to its circumference:

"It is useless to state the real truth of the matter, as it has no effect on those who are subject to this type of hallucination. They can but be left with the flat earth believers and other such people to whom a theory is dearer than a fact" (Petrie 1931).

Nevertheless, it continues to be legitimate and possible to derive technical and historical information from architectural structures, when the material is treated properly within its cultural context (cf. Carlotti 1995), and had Petrie had access to the more up-to-date information now available, he may well have persisted in making sure that the facts were more widely accepted.

As Miroslav Verner wrote: *"the ancient Egyptians' constructions are the best evidence of their mathematical capabilities"* (Verner 2003: 70), and this gives clear support for an approach that has previously proved productive and effective, that of analysing Egyptian architecture from a mathematical and geometric standpoint. Other famous Egyptologists have advocated this approach, for example, in 1865, Richard Carl Lepsius, the famous German Egyptologist wrote regarding the derivation of historical information from architectural remains in Egypt:

"The most likely occurrence of dimensions with a round number of cubits might be expected to be found in rooms, such as the funerary chambers inside pyramids, and there is no doubt that this assumption is right in many cases. The true situation will reveal itself if we collect the measured dimensions of such rooms and reduce them to the length which appears most probable for the cubit, 0.525m" (Lepsius 2000).

Chapter 5.   Arguments from authorities

Although Lepsius's figure for the cubit was very slightly too long, his prediction regarding the importance of pyramid funerary chambers for providing mensuration data was confirmed by the young Flinders Petrie less than 20 years later. When Petrie carried out the first high accuracy theodolite survey of the Giza plateau pyramids he included detailed surveys of the burial chambers, and it was the King's Chamber of the Great Pyramid that provided the most accurate data concerning the royal cubit. This survey marked a milestone in our understanding of Egyptian architecture, as the facts finally began to be distinguished from the fiction.

It is not, however, enough to understand the geometry of these buildings from a numerical or proportional standpoint, or to interpret them as a set of numbers. It is vital to understand the cultural context in which the technical systems were being developed and the religious architecture was being built, and to do this, it was necessary to go back and look at the Ancient Egyptian's society and their daily lives. The Great Pyramids were just one aspect of an incredibly successful and creative state formation process, and so to understand the architecture of their afterlives we need to understand the every day lives of the people that built those structures.

We need to understand that what we are dealing with here is important and sacred Old Kingdom ritual and tradition, and so a level of respect is required on our parts when approaching the subject matter. Only then can we fully understand and appreciate what they could do, and what they did. After all, even our basic number systems are still based on what these giants achieved. Even Euclid was standing on giant shoulders.

6. Archaeology and philology; fieldwork and deskwork

"He used statistics the way a drunkard uses lampposts - for support, not illumination." Andrew Lang

This chapter is included for reasons of academic completeness. In it, I criticise problems with some of the most significant individual works that touch upon this subject, while simultaneously attempting to build up a more general history of the reasons that this problematic scholarship emerged. This chapter is therefore not directly related to the Old Kingdom Egyptians at all, nor is it related to correctly interpreting their achievements. It focuses on the main sources of errors and biases that have impacted on 19th and 20th century scholarship relating to this subject matter. As opposed to archaeology or Egyptology, this sort of approach is often referred to as historiography.

Neither the archaeological material recovered nor the textual evidence surviving from the Old Kingdom constitutes anything approaching a complete record of Old Kingdom knowledge and abilities. The two bodies of evidence, as well as being fragmentary and in many places simply non-existent, are also not apparently congruent, according to mainstream academic literature. In other words, the archaeological conclusions often contradict the text-focussed conclusions and vice versa, and from a logical standpoint this situation is untenable.

In both fields evidence exists that is not attested to in the other. For example, conclusions reached by the Egyptologists from excavations and surveys have not, in the cases studied here, always been in accord with the conclusions of the text-based scholars. The reasons for this are highly complex, but the historiographical approach can help explain why this situation has arisen.

One of the most conspicuous areas of difference is between the archaeology-based interpretations of Egyptian architectural abilities made by the Egyptologists, and the mathematical/textual based interpretations made by the philologists. The Egyptologists included Petrie, Edwards and Verner, while the text-focussed philologists included such academic figures as Professor of the History of Mathematics at Brown University, Otto Neugebauer (1899-1990), and Professor Richard Gillings of the University of New South Wales and Brown University.

The main problem is firstly that the archaeological based conclusions reached by Professor Flinders Petrie, and the others in the field, were never adequately understood, addressed, or referred to by the textual philologists at all. This is particularly notable in philological works written after Petrie's death in 1942, despite the fact that Petrie's familiarity with the architecture of Old Kingdom Egypt, as well as the content of the mathematical texts, was second to none.

In his later years, Petrie was notorious for ignoring the work of other archaeologists, but this does not absolve modern archaeologists and mathematical historians from a responsibility to process the facts that Petrie brought to light in the field. One of the historians who did not seem to fully familiarise himself with Petrie or Edwards's works was Otto Neugebauer.

As one of the principal authorities in the text-focussed armchair world of the 'sciences of antiquity', the opinions of the German born American philologist Otto Neugebauer, regarding the technology of Ancient Egypt, have been highly influential. Neugebauer did not excavate in Egypt at all, and seems from his bibliographies not to have been familiar with some of the fundamental archaeological reports and publications relating to the technology and knowledge base of the Egyptians. Nevertheless, he was influential in developing mainstream perceptions of their skills due to his well known knowledge of the wider field in general, and his knowledge of the textual evidence in particular, including from Mesopotamia and Greece. Furthermore, Neugebauer's prodigy was Richard Gillings, who subsequently wrote one of the standard texts analysing Egyptian mathematical papyri, '*Mathematics in the Time of the Pharaohs*' (Gillings 1982), but neither Gillings nor Neugebauer seems to have been at all familiar with Petrie's work or his conclusions, or the work and conclusions of other Egyptologists such as Somers Clarke and Engelback (Clarke and Engelbach 1991). In particular, '*Wisdom of the Egyptians*' (Petrie 1940) is not referenced in any of their works, yet contained Petrie's most comprehensive synthesis of the facts he had recovered over 70 years surveying and excavating in the field. Finally, both Neugebauer and Gillings even seem oblivious to the statement of I.E.S Edwards regarding the circular symbolism of the pyramids, yet Edwards is widely considered to have been possibly the single most important authority on the pyramids of Egypt during the 20th century, by figures as well known in the field as Dr Mark Lehner.

Figure 54 Neugerbauer and Petrie – Top philologist and top archaeologist

Chapter 6. Archaeology and philology, fieldwork and deskwork

Despite the evidence from the architecture and archaeology uncovered by the Egyptologists in the field, Neugebauer was still able to write:

"The reader may have missed a reference to the astronomical or mathematical significance of the Pyramids.... ....Important mathematical constants, e.g. an accurate value of Π and deep astronomical knowledge, are supposed to be built into the dimensions and structure of this building. These theories contradict flatly all sound knowledge obtained by archaeology and by Egyptological research about the history and purpose of the pyramids" (Neugebauer 1969).

As we have seen in the previous chapter, the evidence did not contradict theories showing that a precursor version of pi was indeed used by the Egyptian architects.

Neugebauer used the phrase 'purpose of the pyramids' in the quotation above, and lower down in the article from which this quote was taken he also referenced another article by the British archaeologist Mortimer Wheeler (Wheeler 1935). Wheeler's article was itself entitled 'Pyramids and their Purpose'. In Wheeler's article he listed a huge amount of architectural data from many pyramids, yet his analysis did not reach any real conclusions, and did not accord with the conclusions drawn by Petrie in the original excavation and survey reports. Petrie nevertheless re-iterated his own conclusions, and further synthesis the data, a few years after Wheeler's article was produced (Petrie 1940: 27 - 31), but Neugebauer seems not to have been aware of these facts at all. Petrie's '*Wisdom of the Egyptians*' (1940) really provided the most complete and accurate archaeological and cultural analysis of the data from Giza and elsewhere in Egypt, based as it was on his vast experience and access to all of the texts and facts, yet Neugebauer does not reference this work at all.

Wheeler's article also did not accord with the later conclusions reached by I.E.S. Edwards (Edwards 1979: 269), which have already been quoted above in chapter 5. Both Petrie and Edwards considered the circular symbolism in the Egyptian architecture to have been part of the builders' original designs, yet this was never even commented on by Neugebauer. It should be noted again that Petrie and Edwards were both considered principal authorities regarding the Pyramids of Egypt and the material culture of Egypt, and whilst argument from authority is not admissible in isolation, when taken in conjunction with the supporting data, the facts of the matter as established by these authorities, and others, become clear, and it is equally clear that both Neugebauer and Gillings were ignorant of some of those facts.

If Neugebauer was indeed ignorant of the conclusions reached by Petrie in his work '*Wisdom of the Egyptians*', and of the equivalent views held by Edwards regarding the circular symbolism, then this is extremely unfortunate. As a result of these omissions, very few people after Neugebauer, including his prodigy Gillings, therefore seem to have been aware of Petrie's excellent analytical work in uncovering the facts regarding Egyptian circular symbolism in funerary architecture. The archaeological evidence, facts and conclusions have therefore never been taken into proper account when historians of mathematics have considered the developments made in Ancient Egypt. This is why the archaeological facts, evidence and conclusions from the field have never been properly synthesised with the textual based data from the mathematical papyri.

By following Petrie's references in all of his publications, it has also been possible to establish, and clearly demonstrate, that Petrie himself was fully aware of every mathematical text from ancient Egypt that has ever been recovered and translated, (save one still disputed alternative interpretation), and so Petrie's conclusions must be given the full weight that they deserve, and are not inferior to those drawn by the textual specialists or more modern mathematicians. Petrie was a superb mathematician himself, as can be seen from his report of the three-dimensional theodolite survey of Giza he carried out almost single handedly, and calculated out entirely by hand.

A gap still exists then between the philological-textual world and the archaeological-material world, especially where Egyptian mathematics is involved. This is surely in part why so many publications now exist speculating on possible explanations for the apparently anomalous evidence that has clearly not been successfully reconciled for Giza. Gillings (1982) did make some valiant attempts to reconcile the cultural evidence from the material artefacts, such as the cubit rules, with the textual mathematical papyri he was so familiar with, but he failed to recognise and incorporate the information from the archaeology of the architecture, produced by Petrie and others, into his analysis.

Perhaps in part because of the sheer magnitude of the task of familiarising one's self with the architecture of ancient Egypt in any depth, or perhaps due to Neugebauer's influence, Gillings never addressed the architecture in his book on Egyptian mathematics.

One phrase in Gillings' otherwise excellent publication goes some way to showing that he never ventured to address the archaeology of the architecture, or the extensive surveys of the architecture and excavations in any in-depth manner. He writes (Gillings 1982) (referring to Piazza Smyth, the 19th century 'pyramidologist') that *"...Smyth asserted that half the distance around the square base of the Great Pyramid divided by its height was exactly equal to π, the ratio of the circumference to the diameter of a circle; and that 1/360 part of the base equals one five-millionth part of the earth's axis of rotation, whatever that might mean !"*.

Gillings therefore 'rubbished' Smyth's whole position, including the fact that the base to height ratio of the pyramid was designed to the same proportions as a

Chapter 6. Archaeology and philology, fieldwork and deskwork

circle's diameter to circumference, or as he puts it, equal to π. It is quite astonishing that Gillings should only lump the more reasonable proposal alongside a 'straw man' remark regarding a different and ridiculous proposal that discredits it by association. Gillings therefore effectively 'threw the baby out' with the associated bathwater. He did not properly address the data from Petrie's most extensive survey of the Giza Plateau available at the time, or the data and conclusions drawn from Meidum.

Gilling's venture into the world of Egyptian circles was limited to an analysis of the surviving textual examples dating from the early Middle Kingdom, detailed on pages 139-153 of his otherwise excellent book '*Mathematics in the Time of the Pharaohs*', which discussed several interesting examples calculating the areas and volumes of circles and circular forms. These examples are mostly taken from the Rhind Mathematical Papyrus (from c.a.1650 B.C., copied from an original from c.a.1850 B.C). Several of the ancient problems (pRhind problems 41, 42, 43, 48 and 50) demonstrate solutions to circular calculations using an effective value of 256/81 (or 8^2 x 4 / 9^2) equating in accuracy to a value of 3.16 for pi, if it had been used. Gillings broadly accepted this value as being the Egyptian value for pi, yet reached this incorrect conclusion from these examples because he did not admit the evidence from the archaeology and architecture, and only observed the textual evidence in isolation.

The reason that this text based value is not effectively a value of pi is as follows.

The Rhind Mathematical Papyrus, which is the most comprehensive of the early mathematical papyri, did not include any method for calculating the **circumference** of a circle, but did include examples for calculating the **area** of a circle. By 'reverse-engineering' these equations, mathematical historians have produced an equivalent Egyptian value of 256/81 for pi, or 3.16, so that the use of the more accurate 22/7 was nowhere to be seen in the texts (Chace 1929; Gillings 1982: 142; Robins and Schute 1990).

This has been taken as evidence that 22/7 (or $3+1/7^{th}$) was unknown to the Ancient Egyptians, but in fact it is nothing of the sort.

The facts, when considered within the Egyptian cultural context, suggest that this area calculation had little or nothing to do with circumference calculations or pi. The area calculation was in fact probably based on an approximate graphical method where a large square made up by 9x9 small squares is drawn out with truncated corners. This truncated form was used as an approximation for a circle, and the number of small squares that fitted inside it could be counted up within the truncated large square and therefore constituted its area (Gillings 1982: 143-144). By way of this method there is no need to assume any relationship with a ratio we now call pi, and so this area method has no bearing on the archaeological evidence concerned with circular perimeters.

As we now know for circles, a circumference $C = pi$ x D, while area $A = pi$ x r^2, so that both individual calculations, for circumferences and areas, can make use if the same stand alone ratio pi, but the Ancient Egyptians, in the Old Kingdom at least, would have been unaware of this. In fact it seems from the archaeological and textual evidence that they had practical and separate methods for each type of problem, for calculating circumferences and areas, and did not realise that a common abstract ratio existed that linked both types of problem. To us it seems normal that pi applies to both circular area and circumference problems, but none of the evidence suggests that the Egyptians knew this in the 2nd or 3rd millennia B.C.

Once more, the value of strictly applying our methodology of thinking like an Ancient Egyptian becomes clear.

Unfortunately there is no example on any of the mathematical papyri from the second millennium B.C. to show us explicitly how they calculated circular circumferences (as opposed to areas), but the hieratic reconstruction in chapter 4 [Figure 53] fits all of the circumstantial evidence.

The only other surviving textual examples of importance are from much later demotic papyri (Parker 1972; Hollenback 1997) of the mid to late 1st millennium B.C., c.a. 350 B.C., and these equations understandably show a more advanced understanding of the relationships between areas, circumferences and diameters, although here the common ratio for pi is approximated to only 3. In fact, although these later demotic examples correctly show the familiar equation $A = pi$ x D^2 / 4, it is very surprising that *pi* is taken as only 3, which is a relatively poor approximation for the time. This is fully 4.7% in error, relatively large compared to the equivalent and much earlier Rhind papyrus error for an equivalent area calculation of only 1%. It seems improbable that this was the best known value for pi known at the time, especially as Archimedes was soon after to define pi down to between 223/71<pi<22/7.

If the demotic example is considered in its historical context, however, it seems that the calculation was what is known to mathematicians as a 'Toy Problem', intended to teach the correct equations, methodology and concepts, whilst simplifying the ratios involved for speed.

Finally, like the Rhind Papyrus, the most famous work of ancient geometry, Euclid's *Elements* (c.a. 300 B.C.), did not include any example for calculating the circumference of a circle

To progress then from this position, it is important to understand that none of these textually attested methods for calculating circular areas imply the non-existence of

Chapter 6. Archaeology and philology, fieldwork and deskwork

other techniques for calculating circumferences, and that the surviving examples may represent only the practice that was best suited to everyday arithmetical use. Nothing on the mathematical papyri precludes a working knowledge that the circumference of a circle diameter 1 cubit was 3 cubits and 1 palm, or otherwise stated, that the circumference of a 7 palm diameter circle was 22 palms. In fact, not only do the papyri not preclude this, but the high level of sophistication shown in the Rhind problems alone would strongly suggest that the much simpler and naturally occurring numbers associated with circular circumference problems were known long, long, before the period from which the papyri have survived.

Gilling's 1972 book on Egyptian mathematics is dedicated to Neugebauer, and the two published other works together, and worked together in the department at Brown University for many years. Neugebauer was for several decades after WW2 considered one of the world's leading lights in the study of the sciences of antiquity, and he was undoubtedly talented. Neugebauer, like Gillings, however, was mostly a philologist, interested primarily in the mathematic texts of antiquity. This focus on the texts goes some way to explaining why neither Neugebauer nor Parker were able to properly incorporate the archaeological evidence from the surveys and excavations that Petrie and others had completed in Egypt. Most orthodox scholars in the postwar period have nevertheless broadly accepted Neugebauer and Parker's conclusions, despite the fact that neither of them was properly familiar with the archaeology or architecture of Egypt.

It is useful at this point to compare the backgrounds of Petrie and Neugebauer, and examine how their origins influenced their later academic conclusions. Although Petrie's father was very religious, he was also an experienced and talented engineer. Petrie's mother was daughter of the first man to map Australia, was also well educated, and so Petrie was brought up with a typical late 19th century Victorian English empirical mentality with a taste for hard work and a hands on approach. For many decades he travelled continually between his sites around the Middle East and his academic base in London, set up for him by Amelia Edwards.

Neugebauer's father was also an engineer, but unlike the empirical Petrie, Neugebauer was educated in the pre-war German academic system that was heavily influenced by the philological tradition. This approach focused on amassing details and prolonged deskwork, as opposed to travel and fieldwork. Originally a student of mathematics, Neugebauer was attracted to the technology of antiquity through work on a publication of the Rhind Mathematical Papyrus, and then through his study of Babylonian mathematical cuneiform tablets. His work displays an impressive attention to detail, but only with respect to what is actually written in the surviving texts.

In addition, the university he worked at between 1922 and 1934, Göttingen, was the central establishments from which the racist theories that supported the National Socialist regime emanated from. There are some good studies that discuss the background of this time in some detail (Arnold 1990; Morris 1994; Marchand 1996; Hale 2004). Whilst he was a superb independent scholar in his own right (Boas 1979), his scholarship demonstrated an ingrained bias against Egypt for the rest of his years; something that is perhaps to some extent echoed in Gillings's works after him.

What is most concerning for today's Egyptologists is that Neugebauer may have exported some of the biases he had inherited from Germany into the scholarship of North America, and from there into that of most of the English speaking world, where it remains to this day. Though always accurate with the textual facts, Neugebauer's interpretation of those against an overarching 'historical trajectory', and his failure to properly address the archaeological facts and data, were problematic. His academic status, influence and the publication of high quality scholarship right into the 1980s has meant that it has proved difficult for new scholars to dislodge his less balanced conclusions.

Figure 55 Hieroglyphics for 'seked', signifying slope angle system

Those following Neugebauer rejected the existence of any mathematical proportions in the pyramid's design, including the circular proportions in the pharaonic architecture (without considering the facts properly or in depth), and attempts were made to explain the proportions of the pyramids entirely with reference only to the simple 'seked' gradients, which we know the Egyptians used, and which are attested in the mathematical papyrus examples. Robins and Shute (Robins and Schute 1990) responded to J.A. Legon's paper (Legon 1990), which had shown how 3+1/7 would have been available to the Old Kingdom Egyptians, by proposing this strictly seked based alternative method, also following J.P.Lauer's calculations (Lauer 1974).

The seked of a slope is similar to its gradient, and is quoted as the number of palms and digits to move horizontally for every 1 cubit rise. The diagram in section 2.3 [Figure 25] shows the seked that corresponds to the slope of the Giza Great and Meidum pyramids.

Sekeds were indeed used to implement slopes on site, but it was incorrect to infer that it was the choice of seked that defined the slope at the design stage. In fact, if the textual evidence is referenced more faithfully, it is clear that for pyramids the seked gradient was in fact defined by the original choice of base/height ratio, and not vice

Chapter 6.   Archaeology and philology, fieldwork and deskwork

versa. The examples on the Rhind Papyrus clearly show that the usual method was to choose the desired whole multiples for the base and height, and then work out from this the seked required to reproduce this on site. Legon duly replied to Robins and Shute to this effect in his paper a year later (Legon 1991). After being calculated from the base and height choice, the seked slope would then have been applied accurately on-site by way of an 'A' frame type balance, with a plumb bob, marked off for the relevant seked slope (cf. Lehner 1997: 210 for tools) [Figure 56].

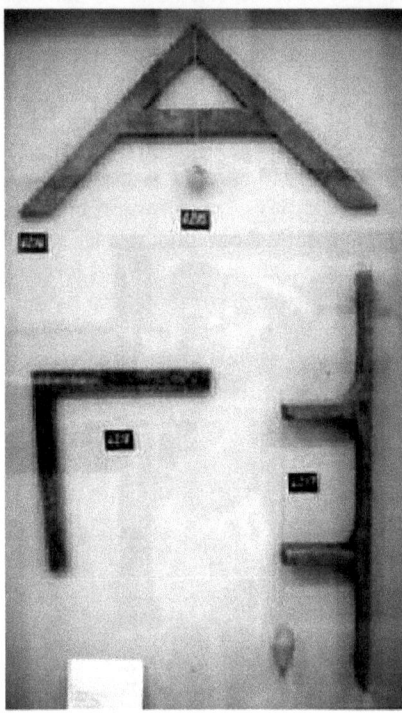

Figure 56 Egyptian construction levelling frames: Cairo Museum

Other surviving documentary evidence for the use of seked gradients includes pRhind problem 56. This calculates the complex gradient of a pyramid with a side-slope of 25/18, which has a base of 360 cubits and a height of 250 cubits (Gillings 1982: 185). This example clearly shows that the Ancient Egyptians were capable of designing to any desired angle at the time it was written, and that it was not any simple seked choice that determined the slope, but the required height and base dimensions chosen [Figure 57].

Interestingly, it has been noted that these dimensions written on the papyrus example are the actual dimensions of the lower 'Bent Pyramid', had it been continued to the top as initially started, and not reduced in slope at the halfway stage. The slope also corresponds to a 'pyramidion' (a small model of the pyramid or also the cap stone), found near the Red Pyramid (Rossi 1999: 222). The photograph below shows the Bent Pyramid with the pyramidion superimposed over it, showing the correspondence more clearly than any written explanation can manage [Figure 58].

As was discussed in Chapters 1 and 2, if the cubit rule was divided into 7 parts to facilitate circumference calculations, then the simple relationship between the seked 5 palms and 2 digits, which corresponds to the symbolic slope as seen in the Great Pyramid and the Meidum pyramid, then the simple seked was really a direct by-product of the cubit rule's 7 part circular origins. The simplicity of the seked value that was produced by this circular relationship was also possibly an additional factor that persuaded the architects to construct Khufu's Great Pyramid at Giza, and the Meidum Pyramid before it, to this form.

The seked theory, when presented as an alternative, did not include the evidence from the papyri that the seked was normally derived from the desired base and height dimensions and proportions. Sekeds were indeed used, but were the product of the proportions, and not vice versa.

Figure 57 RMP Problem 56 – pyramid diagram

Rossi, in the impressive work '*Architecture and Mathematics in Ancient Egypt*', (Rossi 2003), makes the same mistake in accepting the seked theory, but not the evidence that the seked was normally derived from the height and base dimensions and chosen proportions.

Page xiv contains this worthwhile statement: *"In their search for a rule that would explain the proportions of ancient Egyptian architecture, (ppxv) modern scholars have generally ignored ancient Egyptian mathematics and have based their theories on our modern mathematical system"*, but the chapter then reaches conclusions that are directly contrary to this statement, contrary to the evidence from the Rhind Papyrus, and contrary to works by Petrie, Somers Clarke and Edwards, that the seked was calculated from the desired height and base dimensions and desired proportions.

Again on page 216 Rossi claims that slope proportions of 14 and 11 were: *"the consequence of the choice of that Seked"*, completely contrary to what was concluded by Petrie, who surveyed and excavated these structures in minute detail, or for example Legon (Legon 1990). Again, the only written evidence we have shows that sekeds were normally calculated from the chosen dimensions and proportions of the pyramids.

On page 240 Rossi derides those who look for 'hidden' mathematical ratios in Egyptian architecture, yet this is exactly what a large part of Rossi's book seems to be

Chapter 6. Archaeology and philology, fieldwork and deskwork

concerned with. The research focuses on finding the culturally incompatible "golden ratio" in the architecture, and although Rossi eventually correctly rejects this, it is rejected along with the culturally factual circular symbolism, that was found expressed blatantly in the primary dimensions of the structures by some of the top Egyptologists of the 19th and 20th centuries.

There is nothing 'hidden' about the circular symbolism of the Giza Pyramid by any measure. The architects and scribes who created it deliberately expressed the symbolism there, on a huge scale.

The reason for this rejection of the facts is that Rossi is following a similar set of sources to Neugebauer, and like Neugebauer, remained unaware of the conclusions and discussions of the facts carried out by Petrie, Somers Clarke and Engelbach, I.E.S, Edwards and others.

Figure 58 Bent Pyramid with pyramidion found near Red Pyramid superimposed

Rossi may have unsuccessfully looked for the golden ratio 'phi' in the architecture of Egypt, but even more unsuccessfully failed to recognise the very real existence of the proportions of the circle. It may be exactly this sort of persistent failure to acknowledge the real historical facts that leads others to speculate more wildly, as they are disorientated by the uncertainty into which the subject has been thrown.

Finally, on page 67, Rossi writes: *"However, does it really make sense to talk about the approximation of a concept or a number that did not exist in the Egyptian mind?"*, but what Rossi has effectively done here is to extrapolate the legitimate point that the Egyptians did not know pi as we do today, towards a wider, and false, claim that the basic numerical proportions of a circle were not known to them.

The Great Pyramid and the Pyramid of Meidum, and others, were designed by the fourth dynasty Egyptians to have their height to base perimeters proportioned to be the same as the radius to circumference proportions of a circle. The seked was then derived from these proportions for construction purposes. It is also worth remembering that the actual letter and concept of pi have no definitive or exact mathematical definition at all, and effectively cover a whole raft of different concepts, so it is ultimately futile to argue whether or not knowledge of circular proportions constitutes knowledge of pi.

It can certainly be effectively argued that knowing that the circumference of any given circle is $3+1/7^{th}$ times its diameter is to know a good approximation for pi, whereas there is no suggestion here that any greater degree of accuracy or knowledge of the algebraic nature of an abstract ratio pi was in the possession of, or required by, the Egyptian scribes.

In a similar vein to Rossi, Neugebauer and Gillings's works is that of Herz-Fichler (Herz-Fischler 2000), called 'The Shape of the Great Pyramid'. This is a book dedicated to discussing all of the various theories put forwards over the years to explain the proportions of the Great Pyramid. The book contains some excellent information, and a lot of it, but unfortunately arrives at the wrong conclusions in exactly the same way as Rossi, Neugebauer and Gillings did. Again, there is no reference to Verner, Somers Clarke and Engelbach, or Edward's conclusions regarding the circular proportions, even though the pages 70-77 seem to be an attempt to compile a complete list of all those authors who have held this view. The list in chapter 9 (67-77) includes Petrie as one of those who held this view, yet he fails to add that Petrie (Herz-Fischler 2000: 75) certainly concluded that the circular proportions were deliberately used, and maintained this position until his death (Petrie 1940: 30). In fact, a discussion of the sources in the notes to this chapter (Herz-Fischler 2000: 224) clearly demonstrates that although Herz-Fischler seems to have been aware that Petrie had discussed this issue in more depth, from references in other works, he was never able to locate the source of the data, which was in all probability Wisdom of the Egyptians (1940). If we consider that any thorough search of a good library catalogue would have quickly revealed the existence of this work by Petrie, then this omission has to be considered a serious flaw in Herz-Fischler's otherwise impressive book. As a result of this omission he writes "I do not know if this means that late in his long career Petrie had eliminated the pi-theory as a possibility" (Herz-Fischler 2000: 75). The answer to this question is that he did not eliminate it at all (Petrie 1940: 30).

It is unclear from this work if circular proportions were considered to constitute a 'pi theory', because Herz-Fischler never defines exactly what this would mean outwith our modern system of mathematics. He did not consider the actual abilities of the Ancient Egyptians within their cultural context in any depth at all, except in a very short Part I entitled 'The Context', which runs to only 13 pages, whereas Part II, which discussed the various mathematic theories, runs to 136 pages. The reason for this may be partly because, as Herz-Fischler admitted in the Acknowledgements: "The reader should

Chapter 6. Archaeology and philology, fieldwork and deskwork

keep on mind that my studies were in engineering and very abstract mathematics" (Herz-Fischler 2000: xi).

Ultimately, to complete a chapter dedicated the historiography of the pi theory of the Great Pyramid without including either Petrie's work comprehensively, or discussing the details of incorporating the proportions of a circle into architecture in some real depth, as for example were included in Petrie's 1883 survey and 1940 book, seems somewhat negligent.

Petrie already included a discussion of all the main theories proposed for the design of the pyramid way back in 1883, and concluded that the circular proportion explanation was the only one worth commenting further on. After his work at Meidum (Petrie 1892), which supported his conclusion from Giza, he became quite certain that the symbolism was intentional, and by the time '*Wisdom of the Egyptians*' and '*70 years in Archaeology*' were published he was quite clear that these were the facts of the matter. Herz-Fischler certainly seems to have been aware of the survey and the 1892 Meidum report, (Herz-Fischler 2000: 75), but not the later assimilation, synthesis and analysis of all the data in *Wisdom of the Egyptians* 1940.

Furthermore, in chapter 5 Herz-Fischler also treats the seked theory as a separate one from the analysis of the circular proportions discussed in chapter 9. In reality, the seked would have been used to apply the desired circular proportions on site as was discussed above, and so they were part of the same process. Again, this is due to the influence of Robins and Schute (1990) who proposed that the seked theory explained everything, whereas in fact it was considered in isolation from the other cultural evidence and associated archaeological facts.

Finally, Herz-Fischler discusses some philosophical considerations and theoretical premises that any theory would supposedly have to satisfy to be acceptable, including that any theory would have to be applicable to every pyramid (Herz-Fischler 2000: 138). Plainly it would have helped us had the Egyptians decided to use one simple rule for designing every pyramid, but all of the cultural evidence from the archaeology suggests that every pyramid was a new expression of traditional ideas and developing constructional technology, and that each seems to have been personalised for the pharaoh it was built for. Herz-Fischler's premises are therefore fundamentally flawed and not related to the cultural context. Only by understanding the mastabas and pyramids as individual projects, within an ongoing historical development, can the elements of the symbolism be correctly interpreted in each new incarnation. Herz-Fischler was looking for one over-arching master theory in the way text focussed philologists and mathematicians have always done, and in the absence of finding one he incorrectly concludes that only slopes that were '*aesthetically pleasing and feasible from a construction viewpoint*' were what defined the proportions. These were certainly influential factors, but

they were not the only issues that determined the slope choice. Unfortunately for Herz-Fischler, the state of his archaeological and cultural knowledge did not let him arrive at any definite conclusion beyond these (Herz-Fischler 2000: 168). This is a disappointing end to a book that has some excellent and well researched content, but more worryingly, the erroneous conclusions have now also been followed and referenced in other recent works such as '*How the Great Pyramid was Built*' (Smith 2004), further replicating the flawed philological conclusions.

It is necessary, for completeness, to include another reference here to a work by the French architect, Egyptologist and excavator of the Saqqara step pyramid J.P. Lauer, published in 1960 called: 'Observations sur les Pyramids'. This included two chapters discussing the slope angles of the pyramids, and examined whether the proportions of the Great Pyramid had any particular mathematical or geometrical significance. Like Neugebauer and Herz-Fischler, Lauer adopts the stance of the mathematicians and philologists, number crunching the known data, rather than looking at the cultural context in which the possible relationships occurred (Lauer 1960). This is not surprising, as Lauer was in fact originally trained as an architect rather than an Egyptologist, although he certainly developed into a very competent Egyptologist over the years. He writes (Lauer 1960: 6): "This fraction 22/7 corresponds exactly with the upper limit given for an approximation of Π by Archimedes, and so one can justifiably ask if it were not from Egypt that he could have obtained this value. In any case, this value of Π only approaches the real value of Π to the second decimal place, and not to the fourth place, or 3.1416, as was stated by l'Abbé Moreux. He arrived at this figure by taking inexact values given by the Savants [experts/ academics/ scientists] of Napoleon's Expedition to Egypt at a time when the clearing of the rubble from the pyramid was insufficient to permit a precise determination of the thickness of the casing and the position of the corners of the base plan".

Despite this relationship being accurate 'only' to the second decimal place, Lauer then states: "The different relationships that we have evaluated are therefore essentially functions of the slope, which is close to 52°, that was adopted for the Great Pyramid. But can we deduce that these were the actual relationships that determined the choice of this angle? For our part, we don't believe it. It seems much more reasonable to admit that, as Texier wrote: "the essential factor that determines the slope is the lateral edge, as the shape of the corner stones depend on this, and these are erected first and so always dictate the erection of the core and the facing" [Author's translation]. Lauer then commenced to analyse the slope of pyramids based on the 'lateral edges' [the sloped edges up the corners of the sides], which equates, for the Great Pyramid, to a ratio of 9/10 (Lauer 1960: 12).

This unusual explanation is possibly due to his architectural background which influenced him to search

Chapter 6. Archaeology and philology, fieldwork and deskwork

for a practical explanation, but which was based on an unproven assumption that the corner stones were placed first.

In conclusion, there was really nothing new in Lauer's analysis that was not addressed in Petrie's discussion of the various theories, in his report of the 1883 Giza survey, including the 9/10 slope angle (Petrie 1883: 184). Lauer included references to sekeds, but, like the others, he ignores the evidence from the Rhind papyrus that the seked and the face slopes were determined by the height and base dimensions choice, and not by the 'lateral edge' slope or by the seked itself.

In his defence, Lauer would not have been aware of Legon's works showing the significance of the layout plan of Giza as a whole, and he also did not seem to be aware of the significance of the perimeter length of the Saqqara temenos wall that he had partially reconstructed. More seriously, however, he did not seem to be aware of Petrie's published and complete analysis in '*Wisdom of the Egyptians*' (1940), or the opinions of Somers Clarke and Engelback, despite quoting from other parts of their work. As he was working in the post war period the work of these pre-war scholars was slightly anachronistic, and so he can be forgiven in part for these omissions.

In summary, Lauer effectively threw the circular baby out with the theoretical bathwater, and adopted instead a completely un-evidenced explanation based on the lateral/corner edge slope.

Other important or well known works that failed to reach the facts of the matter are '*The Riddle of the Pyramids*' (Mendelsshon 1974: 73), which resorted to an archaeologically un-evidenced procedure involving rolled drums, suggested to Mendelsshon by an electrical engineer, in which the relevant proportions could have been incorporated inadvertently into the pyramid structures. Surprisingly, this speculative and un-evidenced procedure was accepted by one of the modern authorities on Egyptian symbolism, R.Wilkinson, as the correct explanation that explained away any symbolism related circular proportions. This was stated in his otherwise excellent work entitled *Symbolism and Magic in Egyptian Art*, in the section which discusses the symbolism of numbers (Wilkinson 1999: 127), but it is perhaps forgivable when one considers the complexity of the archaeological facts that need to be grasped regarding the subject before reliable conclusions can be reached. It is also necessary to include '*Secrets of the Great Pyramid*' here, (Tompkins 1971), which descended into mysticism, and which was compromised by a rambling chapter by Stechinni, whose ideas were famously bizarre to say the least. It's not quite clear what the conclusions of Tompkin's book were, although it is an excellent read and full of useful information.

The debate over the mathematical skills developed by the Egyptians was also swept up into a more serious and very acrimonious discussion that developed during the 1980s now referred to as the 'Black Athena' debate. This debate related to a book of that name written by Professor Martin Bernal, grandson of Egyptologist Alan Gardiner, which detailed a thesis that called for a reinterpretation of the history of the Eastern Mediterranean Bronze Age, with new emphasis placed on the importance of maritime migration from Egypt and the Levant to Greece in the 2nd Millennium B.C. (Bernal 1987).

Figure 59 Martin Bernal: Author of 'Black Athena'

In support of his thesis, Bernal carried out an impressive and in-depth analysis of western scholarship regarding antiquity, and identified several issues of serious concern. Bernal correctly identified that there was a problem with the current mainstream understanding of the scientific capabilities of the Egyptians, and more specifically, relating to the architecture of the pyramids. He attacked Neugebauer as being partially responsible for this, but as his own understanding of ancient Egyptian technology was in fact mostly based on Neugebauer's work, and those that followed him, he was unable to identify what the problems actually were.

Commentators brought in to defend Neugebauer and attack Bernal could also only refer to the same philological works based on the textual evidence that Neugebauer had produced himself, and so none of the participants were able to refer to the actual relevant archaeological survey reports and material facts produced by Petrie, as they had never been properly analysed or referenced by Gillings, Bernal or Neugebauer, None of them were even aware of Petrie's discussion from 1940, or the conclusion he had drawn and explained, and the facts he had detailed within it. The real facts of the matter were therefore never actually discussed during the whole debate, which descended into a decade long acrimonious, ad hominem filled argument, mostly recycling the old philological, text based, conclusions and biased viewpoints that Neugebauer had reached many years before (Palter 1996: 209-256; Bernal 2001: 247-281).

It is not intended to revisit this debate in any more depth here due to lack of space and time, and because it became associated with an un-related academic incident whereby accusations of racism and anti-Semitism were made that

Chapter 6. Archaeology and philology, fieldwork and deskwork

eventually led to legal action being taken (Lefkowitz 2008). Nevertheless, it is relevant to include a passage from one of the main players in that incident, Mary Lefkowitz, who has argued strongly against aspects of the importance of Egyptian influence on Greece, on the basis that this is not factual but is 'Afrocentrism'. Even she, one of the most vigorous sceptics regarding the accomplishments of the Egyptians, was prepared to accept the reality that the Egyptians developed skills which included an understanding of the ratio Pi. In an online version of an article from 2000 she writes: "In assessing Egyptian accomplishments in mathematics, scholars have tended to adopt a somewhat condescending attitude towards Egyptian methods. They have suggested that the Egyptians were practical men, who could measure accurately, while the Greeks developed abstract theories that made the principles behind the calculations accessible to all. While such assertions are true, they do not tell the whole story. It is clear that while the Egyptian scribes had not developed a special language to describe what they were doing, they did understand that certain types of calculation had universal application, and developed methods and formulas, such as the ratio for determining the circumference of a circle, which closely approximates the value of *pi* (Gillings 1972, 233)" (Lefkowitz 2000).

In fact, in this case Lefkowitz is incorrectly assuming, from Gillings's work, which she references above, based on the texts only, that the Egyptians effectively had a stand-alone ratio that was a rather inaccurate approximation for pi. In reality the Egyptians did not have an abstract mathematical 'ratio', but did have very accurate values for calculating circular circumferences based on $3+1/7^{th}$, as is evidenced in the architecture. What she, and Gillings, effectively did was to combine two erroneous assumptions based only on the textual evidence, to arrive at an approximately correct historical understanding that bore a passing resemblance to the real situation, which had already been derived from the archaeology of Petrie and others. Admittedly Lefkowitz is not a mathematical historian or an Egyptologist, but her acceptance that the Egyptians did have something close to pi is still notable, coming as it is from such a strongly sceptical standpoint.

Likewise, for one of the other victims of this debate, Martin Bernal, I feel some sympathy, as he launched himself into the scholarship of the East Mediterranean region because he regarded it as potentially problematic for the world ideologically and politically. While he was clearly right in that estimation, I am unable to seriously evaluate his thesis of extensive Egyptian and African influence on Greece during the Late Bronze Age, as I am not a philologist, but an archaeologist, and a large part of his book is dedicated to evidence based on linguistics. I am nevertheless always interested to note Oriental and Egyptian discoveries in the archaeology from Bronze Age Greece, such as the fragments of armour with the name of Ramesses II on it, uncovered recently from a Late Bronze Age context on the Island of Salamis. By the Iron Age the contact and interaction between the areas was certainly extensive and prolonged.

Finally, a quote regarding this subject matter from a more popular source that seems to have gained widespread circulation among dogmatic sceptics, is from Gardner who wrote: *"If you set about measuring a complicated structure like the Pyramid, you will quickly have on hand a great abundance of lengths to play with. If you have sufficient patience to juggle them about in various ways, you are certain to come out with many figures which coincide with important historical dates or figures in the sciences. Since you are bound by no rules, it would be odd indeed if this search for Pyramid "truths" failed to meet with considerable success."* (Gardner 1957: 178).

This is usually quoted in isolation by misplaced sceptics, but in fact Gardner more correctly added further down the page the following, which is not widely circulated: *"The only Pyramid "truth" which cannot be explained easily in terms of such juggling is the value pi. The Egyptians may have purposely made use of this ratio"*.

His preferred mathematical speculation for subsequently 'explaining this away', however, is based on a misinterpretation of a quote by Herodotus, that was already rejected by Petrie (1883: 184 Para 145 6th case down). Livio as well (Livio 2002: 57), following Herz-Fischler (2000: 100), concluded that the quote, supposedly made by Herodotus indicating a supposed design criteria for the pyramid, based on face areas, was "nothing more than a misinterpretation of Herodotus in John Taylor's by now infamous book" which was called *"The Great Pyramid, Why Was it Built and Who Built it?"* (Taylor 1859). This 1859 book contained a plethora of confusing information and speculation from the era before Petrie's survey of Giza finally settled the issues, and is referred to in some more detail in Appendix 2.

This concludes the literature review of important but flawed books and articles related to the historiography of the Giza plateau's architectural designs. Many, many other works exist, but most follow on along the lines of the above references, and arrive at the incorrect conclusions for any one or more of the various reasons detailed above.

Chapter 7. Conclusions

7. Conclusions

"The meanings of the buildings in the royal cult complexes of the Old and Middle Kingdoms is so multilayered that it cannot be accurately expressed by the conventional term 'mortuary temple', which captures but one aspect of the much larger whole. The overall architectural program of the complex not only provided a burial place for the king but more importantly supplied a framework for the rites that transformed the human and mortal king into an immortal and divine being. The king's supernatural powers could range from mere magical capabilities to divine kingship and union with the gods. His transformation could be achieved by complicated rituals like the Sed-festival, or it could be set in motion by erecting everlasting symbolic architecture that guaranteed the continuity of the king's divine rule" (Arnold 2005: 31).

This chapter summarises the conclusions reached from the previous six chapters. In it, I discuss the information covered so far, look at some of the wider ramifications of the interpretations made, and review the reasons why a synthesis of the textual and archaeological data was never completed before now.

In this monograph I have attempted to present the facts of the matter as clearly as possible, and to outline the methodology I used to extract meaning from this data.

Nevertheless, the remaining work of revisiting all of the many related textual and archaeological sources in order to fully verify these facts will require the efforts of many scholars over a long period of time. My priority at this stage of the research was therefore to present the work that has been carried out thus far as clearly as possible, to allow peer review, analysis and feedback to begin.

I have tried to synthesise the smallest details with the bigger picture, the technical data with the cultural contexts, and the archaeological evidence with the textual sources. As I see it, the situation is quite clear, and I consider the evidence and meanings I have presented to be fact. Nevertheless, it is only by presenting this work to specialists in the various fields on which this subject matter touches that I will be able to obtain the high quality support from the wider academic community that this research now requires.

However, it is possible to tentatively draw some general conclusions from this work as follows:

- The mathematical achievements and abilities of Old Kingdom Egyptian scribes and architects have not been fully understood or appreciated
- The full extent to which Greek mathematics and geometry was a derivative of Egyptian mathematics and geometry has not been fully understood or appreciated
- The full extent to which the philological approach has failed to correctly interpret the past has not been fully understood or appreciated
- The importance of synthesising technical, cultural and archaeological data from Ancient Egypt has not been fully appreciated and is an ongoing task

To recapitulate on the reasons that the synthesis has not yet been carried out, these are as follows. Knowledge of Egyptian technology and mathematics increased rapidly from 1870 to 1900, as translations of the few surviving mathematical papyri became available, and archaeological data from the standing architecture was first systematically collected and published. Although attempts were made to produce comprehensive publications covering all aspects of Egyptian culture, it was not until 1940, with the publication of Petrie's *Wisdom of the Egyptians* that a synthesis of the technical and archaeological evidence was attempted. Since 1940, very little has been done to advance a synthesised historical narrative that includes the technical detail, despite the fact that progress has been made in separate areas of the field, and at a more general level.

This lack of synthesis in the post-war period was in part due to the growing influence of the text-focussed philological scholars. This situation was exacerbated by the death of Flinders Petrie in 1942, and the marked decrease in archaeological activity across the East Mediterranean region in the post-war era. Finally, the lack of synthesis was also in part due to an ingrained bias regarding Ancient Egyptian achievements that afflicted certain section of academia.

As mentioned in the Introduction, this work attempts to fills the lacuna between Petrie's *Wisdom of the Egyptians* (1942), Gillings's *Mathematics in the time of the Pharaohs* (1982), Edwards's *The Pyramids of Egypt* (1979), Wilkinson's *Symbol and Magic in Egyptian Art* (1999) and Arnold's *Building in Egypt: Pharaonic Stone Masonry* (1991).

Hopefully, this work has gone some way towards synthesising the valuable information within all of these fine publications, and advancing our understanding of the meanings behind Ancient Egyptian architectural symbolism.

With respect to mathematical abilities, the facts of the matter are that the Egyptians were clearly able to manipulate two and three-dimensional geometric forms, and calculate areas and volumes by the Old Kingdom. They were also able to design stone structures architecturally, and build them using standardised units of measurement, with carefully measured slopes and dimensions.

Chapter 7. Conclusions

The cubit was symbolically and technically related to the circle, which was an important symbol for the Ancient Egyptians, particularly within their royal funerary monuments where it represented a protective perimeter, sometime represented artistically as a Shen ring. Accurate approximations for solving geometric problems were available, and could be manipulated with confidence when working with circular perimeters, square roots, areas and volumes.

Furthermore, it is certain from the evidence that the late third and fourth dynasty Egyptians knew that a circle with a radius 7 palms has a quarter-circumference of 11 palms, and therefore that a half-circumference is 22 palms and a whole circumference is 44 palms. The relevant proportions and the numbers themselves, in whole cubits, appear again and again expressed in the primary perimeter dimensions of their pharaonic funerary architecture.

We can see from the various 'sizes' in which the architecture expressed these proportions that they were able to scale the symbolism up by multiplying by factors of their choice. This means that they were effectively able to calculate the perimeter of any circle based on the numbers 44, and 22, and 11 and 7, within the limitations of their arithmetical and unit fractional systems. Whether or not this 'constitutes a knowledge of the ratio pi is, in the end, really irrelevant, as the definition of pi itself is not a fixed classification and never was.

What we can say with confidence is that the Ancient Egyptians were the first people in history known to have used the numbers 22 and 7 in conjunction with circular diameters, radii and circumferences, and that they were the first people to be able to apply the levels of accuracy that these numbers entail to the calculation of circumferences.

We can derive more general points from the information covered in this study. Firstly, the development of the pyramids at Saqqara and Giza systematically produced the fundamental systems of mathematics and geometry on which all of the subsequent developments in these subject areas have been built, right down to Greek and Roman times, and even to the present day.

Although there is next to no documentary or textual mathematical evidence surviving from the Old Kingdom, general facts can be, and have been, successfully derived from the archaeology of the standing architecture, but only when the data is read against its material cultural backdrop.

(A few notable exceptions to this lacuna of textual evidence from the Old Kingdom are the 'Saqqara Arch Ostracon' construction diagram, the seked wall slopes recorded on Mastaba 17 at Meidum (Petrie 1892: 36; Arnold 1991: 9; Rossi 2003: 192; Verner 2003: 76 & 77), a few fractions representing contents written on jars, Nile levels recorded on the Palermo stone in cubits, and quantities of gifts, goods and people recorded on a handful of papyrus tables and ceremonial palettes).

The third and fourth dynasties were a period of rapid, almost exponential, growth and creative development centring around Memphis and the Memphite necropolis. While we can still see the evidence of the rapid development of the funerary monuments from that time, it has been more difficult to reconstruct the actual mathematical and geometrical capabilities used by the architects at any given time. With respect to modern scholarship, this situation was not been helped by the confusing and disruptive influences of various speculative and religious zealots, mystagogues, pyramidiots, extreme skeptics and misguided amateurs who were ready to project their own fancies onto the ancient funerary traditions of the Nile valley, or to deny any credit to the Egyptians for their achievements whatsoever.

The reasons for the continuing lack of clarity that has surrounded this subject is surely in part because the conclusions of the archaeologists who worked for so many decades excavating, interpreting and publishing these great sites has not been properly or adequately synthesised with the textual evidence before now.

This requirement for better syntheses is not just restricted to Egyptology, and is becoming more and more of an issue across almost every field of knowledge, as the sheer volumes of information available to academics and amateurs alike increases ever more rapidly. T.E Tihill referred to this challenge in her book on Greek science, with a statement that could be equally apply to Egyptology: *"We need syntheses to prevent the whole world of learning disaggregating into a kaleidoscopic image of shattered fragments. If the advances of any topic are to be communicated outside an increasingly tiny field of scholars working on it, then they must be comprehensible to people outside that specialist field; they must, in short, be translated, whether from an ancient language such as Greek or Akkadian, or from a technical concept such as multiplication, of which there are four different types in Babylonian mathematics [alone]"* (Rihill 1999: 43).

It is now necessary for historians of mathematics to re-examine the reconstructions of the early development of mathematics that they have been using, and consider the extents to which their reliance on texts has distorted their understanding.

The archaeological evidence shows that it is possible to extrapolate some of the examples shown on the Rhind Mathematical Papyrus back from the Middle Kingdom to the Old Kingdom. It is also clear that the mathematical papyri do not evidence all of the capabilities available to the Ancient Egyptians.

Finally, and most importantly perhaps, it is necessary to look again at the extents to which Ancient Egyptian

Chapter 7.   Conclusions

mathematical achievements have been underestimated with respect to their role in shaping the contents of later documents, such as Euclid's Elements from c.a. 300 B.C. Greek historians acknowledged the debt they owed to Egypt for their mathematical instruction, thanks to the Greeks who travelled to Egypt to learn at the temples, such as Pythagoras and Thales. New evidence and these ancient links strongly point to the reality that European mathematics is largely a derivative of Egyptian mathematics, and that the Greeks were quite correct when they stated this in their histories. These issues are discussed further in the appendices that follow.

The high levels of practical precision seen at Giza are matched by the levels of precision available to the Egyptians in their mathematics. Rules of thumb rubbed shoulders with the first proper methods for calculating volumes of three-dimensional geometrical shapes and for manufacturing these forms in stone to a high degree of precision. These were formidable achievements.

Instead of deriding the achievements of the Ancient Egyptians, modern pure mathematicians and text-based scholars would do better to try and better understand what the ancients were actually able to do, and the fundamental importance of the underlying systems that they developed for us. Hopefully, feedback and peer review resulting from the publication of this synthesis will stimulate a renewed effort to uncover the full story.

It was the intention of this monograph to advance this ongoing work far as is possible.

8. Appendix 1: Secondary Issues

"We shape our buildings, thereafter they shape us"
Winston Churchill

This appendix discusses issues of secondary importance that relate to the subject matter. In it, I outline my position and opinions regarding several disparate issues so that the reader may make some use of the information if required.

The book presents only very few cases of applied mathematical symbolism in Egyptian architecture from a huge range of material. This is only scratching the surface of the ancient architects' achievements through analysis of the most explicit and clear examples of the symbolism known today. Many other examples of this, and similar symbolisms, such as the 3-4-5 triangle which determines the slope of Khafre's pyramid [Figure 60], exist. Only through more thorough studies of the funerary architecture of the other pyramids, and in particular by detailed survey of tomb chambers and sarcophagi, will a better understanding of the use of geometry as iconographic architectural symbolism be developed.

Figure 60 Khafre's Pyramid with the Great Pyramid behind

Two other good examples of the use of circular symbolism in the pharaonic funerary architecture of the Old Kingdom exist in the sarcophagus of Khufu's King's Chamber, and in the granite sepulchral chamber of Djoser's step pyramid at Saqqara, which has a section of 3 $1/7^{th}$ cubits square. Unfortunately both are somewhat irregular due to erosion, vandalism and subsidence, and in particular with Djoser's tomb chamber, further survey is required before any definitive conclusions can be reached regarding its accurate as-built dimensions. For this reason the two cases were not included in the analysis here to avoid confusing the presentation of the facts. It is, however, interesting to note again how the sarcophagi, tomb chambers and pyramidal tombs were in many ways often repetitions of the same themes at different scales, so that the incorporation of the same circular symbolism at each scale is not surprising, and should be expected elsewhere.

Finally, it is worth noting here several related but general issues that require a statement of position in case of any confusion. Many of the discussions regarding Egyptian geometry related to the pyramids have included references to the so called 'golden ratio', most notably in recent years in the work by Rossi, in which it was correctly concluded that this ratio was not known or used by the Egyptians (Rossi 2003). In fact, the golden ratio would have had absolutely no practical value for the Egyptians, and was not related to the cultural evolution of their geometry and mathematics in any way. Livio has also shown that this ratio was unknown to the Egyptians and the Babylonians. The reason it seems to have become associated with Ancient Egypt and the pyramids is that the ratio has a naturally occurring relationship with the proportions of a circle, and so that if the proportions of a circle are deliberately incorporated into an architectural form, then the golden ratio 'phi' is observable inadvertently. This is sheer coincidence, and has nothing to do with the Ancient Egyptian architects whatsoever.

Livio writes "The arguments presented by Petrie, Gillings, Mendelssohn, and Herz-Fischler have been available for decades, yet this has not prevented the publication of numerous new books repeating the Golden Ratio fallacy" (Livio 2002: 61) and Livio also correctly notes that "If we have to choose between Pi and Phi [The Golden Ratio] as potential contributors to the pyramid's architecture, then Pi has the clear advantage over Phi." (Livio 2002: 59). The analysis of the evidence that follows this encouraging statement nevertheless falls into all the same philological holes as Gillings and Herz-Fischler's works did regarding the circular symbolism. Again, this is due to the selective set of works referenced in text-focussed circles regarding this subject matter, thanks mainly to the excessive influence of Neugebauer.

It cannot be stressed enough that the circular ratio pi and the 'golden ratio' phi are very different ratios with very different properties and histories, and that they absolutely should not be confused with one another, despite their similar names and Greek symbols. A precursor stage to pi is indeed included in the pyramids through the use of circular symbolism as we have seen, but this has no historical connection to the golden ratio phi whatsoever.

With respect to the use of Egyptian symbolism in other fields, one of the most prominent modern groups to show interest in the geometry of the pyramids of Egypt is that of the Freemasons. It is impossible to properly evaluate the full meanings of the symbolism within their secretive group, as very little clear information is available to the general public, therefore the subject matter is avoided in this book. It is important to mention, however, that symbolic aspects from Ancient Egypt have been deeply intertwined with the history of the development of the Western world we know today, and many influential figures in Western culture have been freemasons, and have also been interested in Egypt. The influence of Egypt on European and Western culture is profound (Curl

Chapter 8. Secondary issues

1994; Adkins 2001; Reisenauer 2003), perhaps most notably within modern architecture.

The example below shows one of the most famous 'modern' pyramids, but many other examples are to be found around the world, such as on the pinnacle of Canary Wharf in London's Docklands business quarter, or at the Pyramid Arena in Memphis USA, or at 'Luxor' in Las Vegas. These are just a few of hundreds of examples in buildings ranging from supermarkets to skyscrapers.

Figure 61 Ancient design in a modern setting: pyramid of the Louvre

Another secondary point of note to include here relates to the recent conclusions reached by R. Gantebrink and J. Romer regarding the architecture of the pyramids (Romer 2007). It is the opinion of the author that although both of these researchers have carried out excellent work related to the Pyramids and Egyptian architecture (including sending a robot into the 'star shafts' reaching out from the King's and Queen's Chambers of the Great Pyramid), their analyses of the engineering and architectural design elements arrive at inaccurate conclusions, as they were not properly based on the Old Kingdom cultural context. As has been seen, the pyramids were surveyed and interpreted to a very high degree of accuracy by Petrie more than a century ago, and Petrie's conclusions therefore still stand largely unchallenged, because they were the correct conclusions regarding what was intended and achieved during the Old Kingdom. They should be used as the foundation for any analysis of the Giza structures, and at the very least should be referenced for the important information they contained.

Finally, it is worth noting that the existence of the symbolism outlined in this book does not negate the possibility of other symbolic aspects being present in the architecture of Old Kingdom Egypt or at Giza itself. It sometimes seems, in fact, as if the Ancient Egyptians had every intention of overlaying as much symbolism into the pharaonic architecture as they could possibly think of.

Chapter 9. Social Context of early Egyptology

9. Appendix 2: Social Context of early Egyptology

"The monuments – pyramids, temples and tombs, statues and stelae – represent the most valuable source for our knowledge of ancient Egypt"

(Baines and Malek 1980: 10).

This chapter looks at the social and academic context surrounding the recovery of Ancient Egyptian mathematics, when European scholars moved from a position of almost total ignorance in 1850, to a fuller yet still very fragmentary understanding by 1940. In it, I look at how the textual and architectural evidence was first uncovered, and at some surprisingly close links between this recovery work and several important social, political and religious issues that were being discussed at the time.

Two main events changed our understanding of Ancient Egyptian mathematical developments. The first was Flinders Petrie's 1880 triangulation survey of the monuments of the Giza Plateau that resolved many of the unanswered questions surrounding the architecture of Old Kingdom Egypt. The second was the earlier discovery and subsequent translation of the Rhind Mathematical Papyrus, between 1858 and 1877, when it was finally first published.

When he first set up his tripods on the dusty sands in the shadows of the ancient Pyramids, Flinders Petrie took with him all of the religious, academic, nationalist and political concerns that influenced people in 1880 A.D. Understanding the context in which he carried out the survey allows us to better appreciate why this event was an important one within the intellectual consciousness of all those who were associated with Egypt and archaeology in the late 19th century. It was not just a key event in the development of Egyptology as an independent academic discipline, it was an important event for Victorian England and European society as a whole.

In the late 19th century, survey and mapping of foreign lands and monuments was more than simply impartial scientific research. It had become an integral part of the imperial domination process. European colonial powers, armed with superior weaponry thanks to the industrial revolution, ideologically, militarily and then commercially colonised, surveyed, mapped and then exploited distant lands. The young Flinders Petrie, although he may not have been aware of it at the time, was in many ways acting out the role of a typical colonial European gentleman, and recreating at Giza, on a small scale, what was happening on a regional and global basis.

Since the Great Survey of India by English cartographic engineers (1800-1843), the process of surveying and mapping of a territory was one of the prerequisites for the colonial rule of that territory. As the 19th century progressed, the 'gaze of the Empire's surveyors' moved from India, to Canada, to Australia and New Zealand, and then finally turned to the Eastern Mediterranean and the Middle East (Home 2006: 2).

British Imperial survey of the Middle East was initiated in the second half of the 19th century to map and record the region in detail, partly as a response to vigorous French activity in the Holy Land and Egypt. The important 'Ordnance Survey' of Jerusalem started in 1864 and was finally published in 1866. The relevance of 'Ordnance' in the title of this work is related to its military value, as maps were required for regions where military action could be envisaged, so that the ordnance shells shot by artillery, cannons and field guns, could be accurately ranged and targeted on enemies. During the survey of the Holy Land, the engineers of the Palestine Exploration Fund managed to triangulate most of what was then called Palestine and this work was finally published in a huge 10-volume edition that recorded and listed not just the geography and topography of the region, but the flora, fauna, geology and archaeology. Anything that could be of potential value to the empire was thus listed and recorded, from mineral resources to crops.

The young Lord Horatio Kitchener (later of Khartoum) was one of the Royal Engineers who worked on this project, and after 1878 Kitchener went on to triangulate and map the Island of Cyprus, following its 'acquisition' by the British in that year. As well as serving a practical military purpose, these surveys and compilations were very much part of 19th century Europe's obsession with collecting, recording and cataloguing almost anything of value from around the world, and with the ideological dominance over these things that this work entailed. The surveys were a way of taking intellectual possession of the land and everything that was in it.

Colonial survey of new territory was therefore very much in the air when in 1880 the 27-year-old Flinders Petrie arrived in Egypt, alone, with his father's theodolites. Unlike the well-trained Royal Engineers of the Palestine survey, Petrie never went to school or university, but quite independently developed an interest, and eventually an expertise in surveying and archaeology, in a large part thanks to his father's influence as an engineer. Petrie surveyed Stonehenge in 1874 with his own equipment, and a number of other Stone Age monuments in the south of England. He compiled the results of the surveys, and by 1877 had his portfolios deposited in the Map Room of the British Museum. Archaeology was emerging at the time from a subject practiced by gentlemen scholars into a subject of professional academic study. Most archaeologists were still amateur, so Petrie's lack of formal education was no bar to his acceptance by those who were interested in the field. Egyptology was just as much an amateur field, and Petrie was fortunate to live at the point where the professional excavator was beginning to emerge and oust the amateur. In fact, in 1880 when

Chapter 9. Social Context of early Egyptology

Petrie headed out to Egypt, there were no academic or professional departments of Egyptology anywhere in Europe. But all that was about to change.

In 1883 the British invaded Egypt by force, and remained there as the occupying power until 1936. While this military domination was very real, Petrie's amateur triangulation survey of Giza, and his professional archaeological excavations that followed, all over Egypt, helped to put England in a powerful position with respect to European academic and ideological domination over Ancient Egypt and the Middle East. In a time when Nationalism was an ever-growing force across the world, the achievements of scholars from different countries became of national significance.

Until then the antiquarian study of Ancient Egypt had remained very much the preserve of the French, who had initiated the European colonial and cultural movement into Egypt in 1798 with Napoleon's invasion. That major event, and the huge publication that stemmed from it (*Description de l'Egypte*) was followed by Jean Francois Champollion's successful translation of hieroglyphic writing in the 1830s. Similarly in the Holy Land, 1863 saw the first excavations in Jerusalem itself, by Frenchman Louis Ferdinand de Saulcy, while 1864 saw excavations by Ernest Renan at the ancient coastal sites of Byblos, Tyre and Sidon, for Napoleon III. De Saulcy uncovered the so-called 'Tomb of the Kings', causing much indignation in England (Davis 2004: 13).

Furthermore, the French had utilised new photographic technology that became available at the time, which lent scientific credibility to their Holy Land projects. Finally, and perhaps most important of all for the region, the French led construction and opening of the Suez Canal in 1869 was something that proved to be a major success, despite its initially slow economic returns. The construction of the Suez Canal was an event of great geopolitical importance that fundamentally affected world trade, and especially the movement of goods around the British Empire. Its location between Egypt and the Holy Land meant that religion, science, politics, nationalism and colonialism all impacted on this great project to 'part the desert' (Karabell 2004), and its completion was no mean feat.

But it was not just the French who were moving into the region in force. In 1869 Wilhelm, then the crown prince of Germany, had taken possession of a part of the old Muristan area of Jerusalem, and the Lutheran 'Church of the Redeemer' was built on the site. It was eventually dedicated in October 31, 1898, with Kaiser Wilhelm II and his entourage in attendance. He was the first western ruler of modern times to go to Jerusalem, and he personally dedicated the new church with much pomp and ceremony. The Germans were moving increasingly close to the Ottoman Empire from the 1870s onwards, and began surveying the area for a railway network in 1871, and building a railway across modern Turkey in the 1880s. This was part of growing efforts on the part of European nations to exploit the available resources of the declining Ottoman Empire as quickly as possible, to accelerate trade profits, and to gain access through the Middle East to colonial areas farther a field. There were plans to extend more of the new railway lines throughout the Holy Land, and there was a perceived risk for the English that the Germans, who were already building in the North, would be awarded the work, and so dominate the Holy Land. The modern reader needs to bear in mind the competitive nationalist lens through which every event was interpreted at the time.

From the 1880s the Germans became the preferred builders of the Hejaz railway, which still connects sites in the Holy Land, Damascus and Medina, and which was originally projected to run all the way to Mecca to the south. The German Palestine Exploration Society (DVEP) came into existence in the late 1870s and the Germans began to show obvious interest in the construction of the railway and also in surveying and excavating the area as a preclude to that construction (Moscrop 2000: 130) Although the English managed to take over the railway work around Palestine, the Turks and Germans later began construction of the 'Hejaz Railway' in 1900.

In response to this French domination of the region and the rapidly growing German influence, the upper middle class of Britain initiated the establishment of the Palestine Exploration Fund (PEF) that was to become one of the most influential organisations in the region for many years. The objectives of the PEF were ostensibly to use modern techniques to support the English view of the Holy Land and the Bible (Moscrop 2000: 68), and the PEF quickly became an organ of Liberal Protestant thought. After 1867, however, it also became an organisation interested in cartography and the military mapping of the region, and for those interested in planning railway routes through the region. Royal Engineers such as Claude Conder and Horatio Herbert Kitchener were often also strongly religious (Jacobson and Cobbing 2005). The Palestine Exploration Fund was in fact one of the first groups to carry out what is now known as 'Biblical Archaeology'. At the time, this was, in simplest terms, a search for 'realia' (Davis 2004: viii). It was an attempt to ground the 'historicity' of the Bible in demonstrable historical reality, and was an attempt to use science to support the bible rather than to attack it, as had been the case for much of the early 19th century.

This approach taken by the PEF with respect to religious ideas, of using archaeological evidence to support the Bible, was also directly related to nationalism and the ideological importance, as they saw it, of dominating the region for England and for the Church of England. By the second half of the 19th century, English biblical scholars had begun to react to a relentless and intensifying ideology of the German schools of theology, who were actively undermining the historicity of the Bible, supposedly from a scientific, text based, standpoint, but more probably due to the underlying influence of racism

Chapter 9. Social Context of early Egyptology

and politics. For many years the German schools had been less interested in the Semitic roots of Christianity, and with its links to Rome, and had been more concerned with the abstract theoretical sides of Christianity, and in particular with the ideas of the apostle Saint Paul expressed during his travels to Greece.

The archaeologists of the English Palestine Exploration Fund began to react against this radical Biblical skepticism regarding the historicity of the Bible coming from the Germanic Schools, and based on an intellectual movement called 'Higher Criticism', by promoting the study of corroborative physical evidence of the Biblical texts in the form of archaeological material from the Holy Land itself.

Shortly after Petrie's survey was completed in 1880, the English establishment also began to challenge the French domination of research in Egypt by founding the Egypt Exploration Fund, in 1883, later renamed the Egypt Exploration Society. The organisation of the new society was modelled on the Palestine Exploration Fund, and The Egypt Exploration Fund was also clearly aware of the importance that research in Egypt could have for other branches of archaeology and theology. The objective of the new society was "to organise excavations in Egypt with a view to the elucidation of the History and Arts of Ancient Egypt and the illustration of the Old Testament narrative, so far as it has to do with Egypt and the Egyptians; also to explore sites connected with Greek History or with the antiquities of the Coptic Church" (Egypt Exploration Fund 1883: 86). Most importantly, the reference to illustrating the Old Testament in the agenda demonstrates the power that theological concerns had in the research of the ancient Near East including in Egypt. The Egypt Exploration Fund eventually aided the work of its sister society, the Palestine Exploration Fund, by providing them with the first excavator of Palestine, Flinders Petrie himself (Davis 2004: 27).

In late 19th century England, publications of the *Society for the Promotion of Christian Knowledge* and the *Religious Tract Society* rubbed shoulders in bookshops with those of the *Egyptian Exploration Fund*.

A browse through some of the names of those on the committee of the Egypt Exploration Fund, listed at the front of their journals, which were edited by Petrie for many years, reveals the importance that the Egypt Exploration Fund eventually attained. Notable names include the Earl of Canarvon, Field Marshal Sir Edmund Allenby, the Reverend Professor A.H. Sayce, and Lord and Lady Arthur J Evans being just a few from a long list of Generals, Colonels, Sirs, Lords, Ladies, Professors and Reverends. The Egypt Exploration Fund was truly a product of the English establishment at the highest levels.

Although he was initially working alone, was not from the upper reaches of the establishment, and was virtually unknown at the time, Petrie's survey became an important event for the advancement of English intellectual ideology outwith the official boundaries of the British Empire. The results were published in 1883, one year after the Egyptian Exploration Fund was launched, and almost immediately after the publication of this survey Petrie became heavily involved with the new organisations.

This was largely thanks to the wealthy and successful novelist and amateur Egyptologist, Amelia Edwards, who quickly (although not immediately) noticed Petrie's talents, and went on to support him financially and administratively throughout his career.

Petrie's excavation works for the Egypt Exploration Fund following his Giza survey were also closely linked to another major intellectual event taking place at the time. This was the great popular, if not academic, success of the German born archaeologist Heinrich Schliemann's excavations at Troy, on the North side of the Mediterranean Sea in Asia Minor. Schliemann's work had demonstrated clearly that physical remains from the past could be used to throw light on ancient texts (Homer), and on the past itself, and more importantly, that a systematic, modern, scientific and professional approach could yield substantial and concrete results regarding ancient history.

In 1874 Schliemann published "*Trojanische Altertümer*", Ancient Troy, to international acclaim, and his work around the Aegean sent shockwaves through Greek scholarship and the Classics as a whole. Despite the fact his archaeological methods left a lot to be desired, his big dig approach, along with his young and attractive new Greek wife, brought glamour and success to the study of the past, and brought the past alive in a way that the arcane discussions of textual minutae could not. Schliemann was setting the agenda, and his prodigious work rate and mobility across the region is astonishing to study, even by today's mass-transit standards.

In the years following his survey at Giza, Petrie started excavating using techniques that had originated from the work at Troy carried out by Schliemann in 1875 and 1880-84 (Moscrop 2000: 154). The basis of the methods was stratigraphic digging, together with dating and cross-dating techniques, using amongst other things pot fragments and pottery sherds to establish dates by analysing the materials, forms and decorations typologically. In time, Petrie became such an expert on the ceramics of Egypt, the Middle East and the Mediterranean, that the local workforce in Egypt labelled him 'the father of pots'.

In a momentous incident, Schliemann in fact visited Petrie during a visit to Egypt in 1887. Petrie reported that he was "very excited about the *Illiad* papyrus" that had just been found at Hawara (Drower 1985: 138).

And so the intellectual and ideological importance of Petrie's excavation and publication work should not be underestimated. By demonstrating that England could

Chapter 9. Social Context of early Egyptology

produce great archaeological excavations as well as the Germans at Troy, Petrie was literally digging for England, as well as digging for history, the Bible and Orthodox Christianity. By 1886 he was excavating Tell Defenna in the Egyptian delta, which he identified with the biblical Tahpanhes from the Book of Jeremiah, and he even managed to locate a mud brick pavement as mentioned in the biblical text, although: "he was a little disappointed to find no stones in the brickwork, which could conceivably be those put there by Jeremiah, but honesty compelled him to admit that he could find none" (Drower 1985: 97).

With his exceptionally prompt publication of this site, and others mentioned by Herodotus, Petrie was doing for Egypt and the Bible what Schliemann had done for Troy. He was bringing the sites back to life, as real, physical pieces of the past.

Petrie's work was also directly linked to some more unusual religious beliefs relating to the Holy Land and the Great Pyramid that were circulating in some European ideological circles at the time, and which today seem rather odd. Since the publication of John Taylor's (1784-1864) complex mathematical work entitled *The Great Pyramid: Why was it Built? And Who Built it?* (Taylor 1859), many of the technical aspects of the Great Pyramid had become embroiled in discussions surrounding the new metric system that was being adopted across the globe. Taylor and his followers, who included the Astronomer Royal of Scotland Charles Piazzi Smyth (1819-1900), supposedly found numerous coincidences between the measurements of the pyramids and the geometry of the earth and the solar system (Smyth 1880). They also concluded (incorrectly) that the British Imperial system of measures (inches, yards, feet) was derived from a far more ancient and possibly divine, system. This theory played a significant role in the debates over whether Britain and the United States should adopt the metric system.

Smyth was also a prominent proponent of 'British Israelism', sometimes called 'Anglo-Israelism', which was the belief that that many early Britons, Europeans and/or their royal families were direct lineal descendants of the Lost Tribes of Israel. Proponents asserted that favor with God was based on one's racial status as an Israelite. The British Israelism theories were apparently older in origin than the 19th century, and had been promoted to justify the break of the Church of England from the authority of the Vatican and the Roman Catholic Church under King Henry VIII, by British theologians claiming that the English were among the Lost Tribes of Israel.

The Astronomer Royal Smyth also claimed, and presumably believed, that the unit he described as the 'pyramid inch' was a God-given measure handed down through the centuries from the time of Israel, and that the architects of the pyramid could only have been directed by the hand of God himself. To support this, Smyth said that, in measuring the pyramid, he found the number of inches in the perimeter of the base equalled one thousand times the number of days in a year

Into this intellectual milieu; and out onto the dusty hot sand of Giza, stepped Flinders Petrie. Although he was interested in Smyth's theories, and although his father had followed them closely, Petrie's legacy to the study of Egypt turned out to be quite secular in nature, as he drew conclusions directly contrary to those drawn by Smyth and Taylor. Despite the military, political, nationalist and religious tug of war that had developed over the Holy Lands and Egypt, Petrie himself, perhaps because he initially worked independently of any official organisation, was somehow able to stand back from all of the ideological issues and produce a remarkably frank, balanced and objective scientific survey report. The report accurately reflected the archaeological remains at Giza, and accurately interpreted the details of the work of the Pyramid builders.

Petrie measured the pyramids, disproved Smyth and Taylor, and established himself as the new authority on Egypt (Moscrop 2000: 154).

"... A new stir arose when one day I brought back from Smith's bookstall, in 1866, a volume by Piazzi Smyth, Our Inheritance in the Great Pyramid. The views, in conjunction with his old friendship for the author, strongly attracted my father, and for some years I was urged on in what seemed so enticing a field of coincidence. I little thought how, fifteen years later, I should reach the "ugly little fact which killed the beautiful theory"; but it was this interest which led my father to encourage me to go out and do the survey of the Great Pyramid" (Petrie 1931: 13).

The survey Petrie carried out at Giza was an astounding quantity of work for one man with so little experience in Egypt to carry out in such a short time. The methodology and accuracy of the work is no less impressive. Even today Egyptologists frequently refer to his survey, which remains the authoritative source for the basic measurements of many of the features of the whole funerary complex.

To survey the plateau with his theodolites, he first set up and accurately measured a base line just to the south of the Great Pyramid, and used this as the basis from which to extend a triangulation network that encompassed the whole plateau. This allowed him to accurately measure it all to within a fraction of an inch. The network consisted of around 14 'stations', and theodolite angles were taken between all of these to various key architectural points on the pyramids and temples, and also back to the points that had already been geographically fixed, such as the summit of the Great Pyramid. The sighting stations were generally set up on prominent outcrops to ensure good visibility, such as the on top of the large tomb of Khentawes and the Mortuary Temple of Khafre's pyramid. Stations to the north of the plateau were

Chapter 9. Social Context of early Egyptology

established along a straight line running SW to NE that may have been set up deliberately in this way to ensure additional accuracy, due to the ease of establishing station points visually along a straight line.

Finally, Petrie even surveyed into the pyramids themselves, by setting up a chain of theodolites penetrating into the deepest shafts and most distant chambers.

The report of all this work was published in 1883 in a book of 250 pages and 16 plates that included a mass of measurement details as well as an extensive and comprehensive historical analysis of the data and theories (Petrie 1883). It was this work that set Petrie up as a scientific authority on the Pyramids, and the work that followed on from this meant that by the end of the decade Petrie was an accepted archaeological expert. By using the experience he had built up over these years, he eventually trained virtually every British Middle Eastern archaeologist until 1935 (Moscrop 2000: 156).

In Palestine as well, Petrie's demonstration of a ceramic typology (dating by establishing a sequence of pottery sherds) at Tell el-Hesi also became the foundation of Palestine archaeology. Later practitioners in the field acknowledged their debt to him. William Foxwell Albright (the great authority in Biblical Archaeology) called him the "Nestor" of Palestinian archaeology and labelled him a genius. In a memorial note after his death, archaeologist Nelson Glueck wrote, "All of us who are engaged in archaeological pursuits stand on the shoulders of men like him who pointed the way which we follow today". In recognition of his valuable contributions to archaeology, Petrie received a knighthood in 1932 (Davis 2004: 30).

The most notable aspect of Petrie's work, however, was his ability to step away from the religious, nationalist and racist ideologies of his time, and to evaluate the Ancient Egyptians and their monuments from an impartial, empirical and scientific point of view. While he was certainly a product of the 19th century, and clearly a man of the British Empire, he also established good long-term relationships with his Egyptian excavators, and worked with people of any nationality as long as they were competent. While the Palestinian Exploration Fund retained its religious raison d'etre right into the 20th century, Petrie was able to interpret the archaeology without being overly influenced by religious concerns, and while Smyth was never able to leave his bizarre theories behind, Petrie was ultimately able to see through the ideology, and establish what the Ancient Egyptians had actually achieved.

When he discovered the only known historical reference to ancient Israel on the 'Merneptah Stele' in Luxor in 1883, Petrie was quick to realise the relevance of the find. He was, however, equally quick to realise just how it would be seized upon by those influenced by religious concerns. He commented that: "This stele will be better known in the world than anything else I have found". A fellow scholar Spiegelberg, who was with him at the time agreed, and commented "Won't the reverends be pleased!" (Drower 1985: 221).

His great supporter Amelia Edwards, however, valued Petrie for his archaeological methods writing: "I feel you are setting a splendid example of scientific excavation to all of Europe…I tell Mrs. Petrie that there is but one W.F.P. and that I am his prophet. I am delighted to be his prophet" (Drower 1985: 80).

In his search for the truth and the facts regarding Ancient Egyptian abilities in mathematics, Petrie was aided by another major event in Egyptology, the discovery of the Rhind Mathematical Papyrus in 1858 by the Scottish antiquarian Alexander Henry Rhind. Although Rhind bequeathed the papyrus to the museums of Edinburgh, it reappeared in 1864 at the British Museum in London where it remains to this day. Before the discovery of the Rhind Papyrus little was known of Egyptian mathematics, and so its discovery and identification was a major event.

The trustees of the British Museum ordered facsimile copies of the papyrus to be made in 1869 (these are carefully drawn copies rather than photographic copies). Work on producing plates of the papyrus also got underway, but was delayed until the archaeologist August Eisenlohr of Heidelberg visited England in 1872, secured copies of the plates, and published the first translation (into German) in 1877.

For the next half century this German translation was the only one available, although specific issues in Egyptian mathematics were discussed in the many journals that circulated at the time, including in the Egypt Exploration Fund's.

During the period that followed, major strides were made in the translation of hieroglyphic writing so that by 1923 a new edition was required, and published, by T.E. Peet, Professor of Egyptology at the University of Liverpool. This new edition included some additional fragments of the papyrus that had been recovered in the New York Historical Society's collection by chance (Cajori 1930: 190). Finally, in 1932 an extensive new version that included details of other mathematical papyri was published by A.B. Chace, Chancellor of Brown University in the United States of America.

In 1940, after all of these translations had been published and widely distributed, along with translations of the other important mathematical text, the Moscow Mathematical Papyrus, Petrie's book *Wisdom of the Egyptians* was published. This took into account all of the details from these papyri, and combined the information with the archaeological and architectural information that Petrie had built up over so many years. This work included a chapter that was effectively the synthesis of all of Petrie's knowledge of Egyptian mathematics, and it

Chapter 9. Social Context of early Egyptology

was in this work that he confirmed that the evidence of circular proportions in the architecture of the tombs was so systematic, 'that we should grant that they were in the builder's design'. By analysing the text of this book, and the references within it, it has been possible to show that he was clearly aware of every single translation of the major geometric problems that had been made from mathematical papyri at the time (other than a disputed alternative interpretation of the unclear Moscow Mathematical Papyrus Problem 10 that has never been verified).

Information from mathematical papyri that became available only after Petrie's times, for instance from the Reisner Papyrus (Gillings 1982: 243), or the Egyptian Mathematical Leather Roll (EMLR) (Gillings 1982: 89), only contained arithmetical information or organisational information, and did not impact on our understanding of two or three-dimensional geometry.

It is therefore possible to say that since 1932 and 1940, very little has really changed regarding our basic understanding of Egyptian Geometry, and that Petrie's conclusions still stand, un-superseded and unchallenged, because they were basically correct. His death in 1942 marked the beginning of a period of relative stagnation in the work to form a synthesis of the architectural and textual evidence.

Although this relative stagnation in the synthesis of the archaeological and textual evidence is lamentable, the more important point is that without Petrie and archaeology, the situation at the time of his death may have been very much worse.

Petrie was one of the main proponents of archaeology and the scientific method, but it is important to understand that the scientific method does not simply mean using expensive or complicated equipment. In archaeology, it is a state of mind whereby one reconstructs a picture of the past from all the available evidence that has been uncovered, and through a systematic analysis of that evidence. Any gaps in the evidence can be partially bridged by using logical arguments to extrapolate from what is known in order to interpolate the unknown. In this respect, real scientific methodology is not overly sceptical in nature. An overly sceptical approach will only consider the evidence that is known, and will not attempt or allow a description of the unknown. This can produce a picture of the past that is badly distorted, as it does not accept that the gaps in the evidence are gaps at all. An overly sceptical approach will consider that absence of evidence is evidence of absence, but in fact this is effectively extrapolating the gaps into the evidence, rather than extrapolating the evidence to bridge the gaps.

In contrast to this scepticism, Petrie's empirical, evidence based, approach aimed to assemble as much evidence as possible initially, and then to extract the maximum information from the body of evidence using logical arguments, cross-dating methods and sequence dating.

Only them would the actual history of the past be reconstructed, and cross-referenced with any textual sources that had survived.

In the preface to one of his most widely read works, Egypt and Israel, Petrie refers to this intellectual tightrope he walked between the sceptics who believed nothing of the Bible was true, and the fundamentalist zealots who believed every word. He writes: *"The purpose of this volume is to illustrate the general historical setting of the narratives of the Old Testament and Christian times; to see how we must understand them as part of the history of the period; to see what consistent conclusions we can reach on taking into account all the circumstances; and to show the point of view of a general historian in regard to these narratives.*

This position has the disadvantages of a middle course. Those whose criticism runs to proving every statement unhistorical, may resent the plain acceptance of documents and statements, wherever not modified or disproved by more certain sources. Even when statements in one part of a document contradict another part, I believe that it may generally be found that the accidental omission of an interval of time, or of a qualifying circumstance, has been the cause of the discrepancy. Misapprehensions and blunders of compilers are far commoner than sheer invention.

On the other hand, those who wish to accept entirely incompatible statements without comparison, may not relish the inevitable necessity of having to yield to historical consistency. They may be ready to revile the errors of a transcriber, while they yet cling to the infallibility of a compiler. Yet there is scarcely any historical statement in the Bible that has not been compiled – generally more than once – out of the editing of earlier documents. Statements which may have been minutely correct as originally written, are sure to suffer when they are subsequently condensed and fused into a more general narrative" (Petrie 1912ii & iii).

Although also based on material evidence, this methodology is completely opposed to the older methodology of the antiquarians and religious zealots, whereby specific artefacts were sought out that supported nationalist and theological agendas and theories. Petrie was not alone in this scientific use of archaeological material to illustrate real history. One of the other well-known proponents of this approach was a founding member of the PEF, the Reverend Professor A.H. Sayce, Professor of Assyriology at the University of Oxford in England (1846-1933). Using archaeological evidence, Sayce "developed and proclaimed a carefully constructed case for the superiority of this external evidence over the internal, philological criteria on which the critics appeared to depend." (MacHaffie 1981: 323). This means

Chapter 9. Social Context of early Egyptology

that he demonstrated that when considered in its wider context, archaeology was a better method of interpreting the distant past than a textual analysis based on critical 'theories' (Sayce 1890; Sayce 1894). Over the remainder of the century an enormous quantity of material evidence was produced from Palestine and Egypt. This was uncovered in bulk by way of Big Dig excavations of the type Petrie was running annually, and reports of the results of these were widely read in England and elsewhere.

With respect to the implications of this archaeological activity for 'the man in the street' in Late Victorian England, by the end of the century "The public believed that a new means of proving the divine nature of the Bible had been sent from heaven to bolster the evidence supplied by miracle and prophecy" (MacHaffie 1981: 321). Clearly, archaeology at the end of the 19th century played such an important role in the public consciousness, and in the shaping of cultural ideas, that it is sometimes difficult to appreciate the full extent of this today.

Sayce, Petrie, the Palestine Exploration Fund and the Egypt Exploration Fund carried on publicly verifying history through archaeology for many years, and by the time the new generation of rich American scholars and philanthropists arrived in Jerusalem at the start of the 20th century, the old English diggers were well ensconced on a mountain of archaeological evidence. The famous American archaeologist William Albright (1891-1971) in fact arrived in the Holy Land as an avid follower of the most radical school of Old Testament Higher Critics, but was rapidly converted on site to the archaeological way by these old dogs of archaeology.

Other new American archaeologists soon arrived in the region, including James Henry Breasted (1865-1935), founder of the University of Chicago's Oriental Institute, who persuaded J. D. Rockefeller to finance the huge new Palestine Archaeological Museum. This was built between 1930 and 1938 and still stands today. In Egypt, George Reisner (1867-1942), Professor at the University of Harvard, dominated the scene at Giza.

These archaeologists, and the archaeological excavations they ran, shaped the intellectual scene for the coming second world war, and in this respect, one final archaeologist, a Scottish born Englishman, should be mentioned here. This was the eccentric and flamboyant Sir Mortimer Wheeler (1890-1976).

Just as Petrie finally passed away at the age of 89 in Jerusalem, in 1942, Wheeler was fighting off General Rommel's 'Desert Foxes' in the crucial battles of el-Alamein in western Egypt, not far from Giza. This one example from many similar events shows clearly how closely intellectual, archaeological, political, religious and military issues remained entwined during the first decades of the 20th century.

As quoted in the introduction, many scholars have used research and study as a means to tackle social issues, and archaeology is particularly effective in this respect: "The history of archaeology is nothing if not the record of a continual struggle by scholars to rise above the biases, preconceptions, and delusions of previous generations….It is also….a distinctive mode of behaviour, in which the participants cannot help but be deeply affected by the hopes, fears, and power relationships of their own societies" (Silberman 1998: 268).

The next chapter looks at some additional social ramifications of the synthesis of textual and archaeological evidence carried out in the earlier chapters of this book. The conclusions that were reached demonstrated greater levels of Egyptian mathematical skill than has been appreciated, and these conclusions now demand that many of the traditional interpretations made by mathematical historians are revised. In particular, the contributions made by the Egyptian scribes to the development of Greek and Greco-Egyptian mathematics, geometry and architecture must be looked at in detail and in depth once again.

For Egypt, it was possible to establish a clear and gradual developmental sequence for the technologies that emerged during the early Old Kingdom, most importantly during the two centuries from c.a. 2700 B.C. to c.a. 2500 B.C. These technologies included agricultural, mathematical, architectural and scribal techniques, and all of these developed simultaneously and were interdependent.

In Greece, there is no such clear evidence for a gradual development of technologies during the Iron Age.

Instead, what is seen during the proto-historical Archaic Period is that useful Egyptian methods were rapidly adopted from 'Saite' dynasty Egypt.

The next chapter looks at some of the mathematical evidence for this transfer of skills, and at some of the issues that need to be re-interpreted and reformed as a result.

Chapter 10. Egyptian and Greek mathematics

10. Appendix 3: Egyptian and Greek Mathematics

"Accurate reckoning for inquiring into the knowledge of all things, mysteries, all secrets"
    Ahmes the Scribe, Rhind Papyrus, 1650 B.C.

This appendix discusses some of the general issues surrounding Egyptian, Greco-Egyptian and Greek mathematics that are related to the subject matter of this monograph. This is not intended to be a fully academic addition, and is only an attempt to identify some of the wider issues that may have to be revisited.

The essential difference is as follows: For the Egyptians, geometry first arose from the fields along the banks of the river Nile. For the Greeks across the sea, geometry first arrived by boat. In this chapter we will look at some of the most important historical issues related to the original development of geometry.

The very earliest evidence of Egyptian hieroglyphic writing found to date is from bone and ivory tags marked with pictorial symbols, and clay seal impressions on pottery vessels, which have been found recently in several Egyptian tombs. These new discoveries date back as far as 3,400 B.C., and challenge, and probably disprove, the old belief that writing in Egypt was a derivative of writing developed in Mesopotamia.

The pictographic tags represent specific goods, places, objects or quantities, and were discovered during excavations by the German Archaeological Institute in Cairo in the tomb of the predynastic ruler Scorpion I (Larkin 1999) at Abydos.

	∩	ᒐ	𓀔	𓏲
1	10	100	1000	10,000
100,000	1,000,000	\multicolumn{3}{c}{2004}
⌇	𓀎	𓀔 𓀔 ⅠⅠⅠⅠ		

Figure 62 Basic Egyptian base-ten hieroglyphic numbering system

The earliest number system known from Ancient Egypt is almost as old as these proto-hieroglyphic seals, and is formed on a base-ten structure whereby individual numbers of objects are represented by single dashes, up to a total of ten, which then has its own sign. The sign for ten, an arched loop, is thought to represent the short length of rope used to tie the feet of cattle together to prevent them from escaping. These multiples of tens along with more single digits can then make up all the numbers from 10 to 99, whereby 100 again has a new sign represented by a length of coiled rope, and so on. The sign for 1000 is a lotus plant, the sign for 10,000 is a finger, the sign for 100,000 is a tadpole, often used to represent very large numbers due to the fact that they are usually found in large groups. Finally, the sign of a seated man holding up the sky, and representing infinity is used for one million [Figure 62]. Although the symbols are different, this system is similar in structure to Roman numerals, and to an early Greek numbering system known as acrophonic or Herodianic after the writer who first described them.

These signs were the principal system used in formal hieroglyphs throughout the dynastic period of Egyptian history, and they can still be found on the walls of many of the temples in Egypt. They are often included as part of offering scenes where large quantities of food or prisoners or prestige goods are offered to the pharaoh to demonstrate his importance. In addition, the coil sign for 100 was used for the linear measurement of 100 cubits, which was known as a 'khet'.

The photograph below is a good example of the early use of the hieroglyphic numbering system in a tomb offering scene, and shows a stele from the tomb of Nefertiabet, a daughter of the Pharaoh Khufu, from her tomb at Giza dating to the 4th Dynasty c.a. 2,500 B.C. (Louvre - E22745).

The stele depicts some of the items placed in her tomb to ensure her comfort in the afterlife. On the far right is an inventory of the clothes and fabrics buried with her, and great numbers of these items, into several thousands, are listed beside the signs for the material [Figure 63].

Figure 63 Stele of Nefertiabet daughter of Khufu

During the Old Kingdom a shorthand version of this hieroglyphic writing system was developed known as 'Hieratic', and this became widely used for writing quickly and compactly in ink onto papyrus or onto pottery sherds known as 'ostraca'. The older Hieroglyphic numerical sign system continued to be used in formal mural inscriptions, such as in tombs and on temple wall inscriptions, but Hieratic rapidly became the

Chapter 10. Egyptian and Greek mathematics

predominant script used for recording and communicating information on a daily basis.

Hieratic numbers were used on the Rhind and Moscow mathematical papyri and on accountancy tables throughout the Middle and New Kingdoms and well into the 1st millennium B.C.

Eventually, during the 25th dynasty (c.a. 700 B.C.), a third new Egyptian script called 'Demotic' appeared in the delta region, and became increasingly important during the 26th dynasty (672 B.C. – 525 B.C.). The 26th dynasty was known as the 'Saite Period' as the capital of Egypt was moved to Sais in the Delta rather than being at the traditional sites of Memphis or Thebes. Despite the fact that the artistic repertoire revived and refined during the Saite period harked back to the earlier dynasties stylistically, it was a time of innovation and change. The new Demotic script was originally the 'business hand' of the Delta region, and was effectively a much abbreviated version of the older Hieratic script (Chrisomalis 2003: 489). Hieratic continued to be used widely in Upper Egypt for some time, while Demotic became the normal script used in the Nile delta region, until it was officially accepted as the preferred script for all Egyptian communications during the 26th dynasty. Hieratic is only found on a limited number of religious texts from that period onwards, however, the new Demotic number system was structurally identical to the Hieratic number system on which it was based.

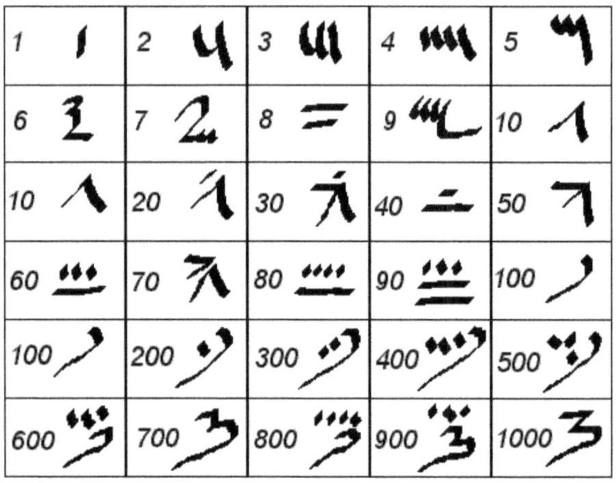

Figure 64 Basic Egyptian Hieratic number system

This official change in the 26th dynasty coincides with a number of reforms that took place at the time relating to measurement, writing and canons of art. It also coincides with the foundation of an important 'emporion' or trading post set up in the Delta for the Greek traders called Naukratis, meaning 'the city that rules over ships'. This key settlement was probably first granted official status during the reign of the pharaoh Psammetichus I, around 650 B.C. and its influence on Eastern Mediterranean cultures cannot be over-estimated. Until that time Egypt had been a heavily traditional and inward looking society, based on many ancient rules and rituals, and had never been particularly open to foreign peoples. At Naukratis, however, the Greeks were able to interact with the Egyptian people and adopt and adapt the skills and knowledge that they learned there for their own purposes. Young Egyptian children were trained as dedicated translators to aid communication between the Aegean peoples and the Egyptians, and this process was possibly in part a deliberate attempt to foster a military alliance between the two regions as well as economic cooperation. The threat to both regions from Mesopotamia in the east was growing at this time. Many temples were constructed at Naukratis in hybridized styles combining traditional and well-developed Egyptian building techniques with Aegean motifs and flourishes. In fact, Naukratis played a central role in the development of the traditional Greek styled temple. Evidence uncovered by Flinders Petrie (Petrie 1886-1888) and other archaeologists who followed him showed evidence of this hybridized eastern Mediterranean style that was developing, in particular the Proto-Aeolic style [Figure 65] which was a precursor stage between the older Oriental styles and the later Ionic, Doric and Corinthian orders that were to become so characteristically Greek (Betancourt 1977; Shiloh 1979).

"Amasis was partial to the Greeks, and among other favours which he granted them, gave to such as liked to settle in Egypt the city of Naukratis for their residence. To those who only wanted to trade upon the coast, and did not want to fix their abode in the country, he granted certain lands where they might set up altars and erect temples to the gods. Of these temples the grandest and most famous, which is also the most frequented, is that called 'the Hellenium'. It was built conjointly by [a long list of Greek city states]… These are the states to whom the temple belongs, and they have the right of appointing the governors of the factory…." (Herodotus Histories II:178).

Figure 65 Proto Aeolic motif from Naukratis, McLean Museum, Greenock

The most importantly single group who traded with Naukratis were the Milesians from the city-state of Miletus in the west coast of Asia Minor/Anatolia. With respect to the historical development of mathematics, two

Chapter 10. Egyptian and Greek mathematics

of the greatest figures in Greek history hailed from the region of Miletus. Their names were Thales of Miletus (c.a. 624 - 547 B.C.) and Pythagoras of Samos (c.a. 569 - 475 B.C.). Various Greek sources tell that Thales learned his geometry from the Egyptians in Egypt where he had travelled. When he returned, he advised the young Pythagoras to go to Egypt, where he studied with the Egyptian priests at the temples in Thebes from 535 B.C. until the fall of Egypt after the battle of Pelusium in 525 B.C., at which point he was forcibly taken to Mesopotamia.

New evidence supports these historical reports, and indicates that the Milesians took the number system they had learnt in Egypt back to the Anatolian coast, adapted it to their own scripts, and spread this system throughout the Aegean during the late 6th and early 5th centuries B.C. The city states that benefited from these systems included what subsequently became the greatest pre-Alexandrian centre of learning, and a city famed for its architecture and design, Athens (Chrisomalis 2003).

Both the number system and the unit fraction system used by the early Greeks show a remarkable continuity of structure with the Egyptian precursors (Chrisomalis 2003: 492), and as the Western systems are based on Arabic and Greek precursors, the Egyptians therefore invented the base-ten number system that we still use today.

1	Ι
5	Π
10	Δ
100	Η
1,000	Χ
10,000	Μ

ΗΗΔΔΔΠΙ = 236

Figure 66 Greek Acrophonic or Herodianic number system

"The Greek alphabetic numerals are extraordinarily important for understanding the history of numeration, but the debate regarding their origin has hardly progressed in a century. Early theories holding that the numerals were developed in the eighth century BC or earlier, or that they, like the Greek alphabet, had a Semitic origin, have now been refuted…The major study of the alphabetic numerals that Marcus Tod had hoped to present in the 1950s was never completed, leaving us with only a single brief paper on the subject from this pioneer (Tod 1950)……. the study of the early history of the Greek numerals (both alphabetic and acrophonic) has generally been ignored in favour of limited studies of regional variations that developed much later…. When they have considered the topic, classical epigraphers have assumed that the alphabetic numerals were independently invented, without considering the possibility that the system had an external origin. In this paper I contend, on the basis of structural similarities and historical indications, that the Greek alphabetic numerals developed from the Egyptian demotic numerals in the context of Ionian trade with Lower Egypt in the early sixth century BC" (Chrisomalis 2003: 485).

The Greeks used two different number systems, the first and earliest being the acrophonic or Herodianic system, which is found in inscriptions and laws since the 5th and 6th centuries B.C. This system was remarkably like the older Egyptian system, and is similar to later Roman numerals. The main difference is that letters represent the sound of the first letter of the number, so that, for example, 5, 'Pente', is represented by a P, or a pi, in Greek. Likewise 10, Deca, is represented by the triangle representing the Greek D, or Delta, and so on. By adding together symbols in order any number could be recorded with a handful of letters. In essence, this is exactly the same as the Egyptian Hieroglyphic numbering system that had been in use for over two thousand years before it appeared in Greece. Only the symbols are different.

ΦΛΘ

Figure 67 Number 539 in alphabetic numbers

The table on the left shows the letters and numbers were used for the different values, and the number at the bottom of the table shows how the individual letters could be built up to represent a larger number [Figure 66].

Alpha	Beta	Gamma	Delta	Epsilon	Zeta	Eta	Theta
Α α	Β β	Γ γ	Δ δ	Ε ε	Ζ ζ	Η η	Θ θ
1	2	3	4	5	7	8	9
Iota	Kappa	Lamda	Mu	Nu	Xi	Omicron	Pi
Ι ι	Κ κ	Λ λ	Μ μ	Ν ν	Ξ ξ	Ο ο	Π π
10	20	30	40	50	60	70	80
Rho	Sigma	Tau	Upsilon	Phi	Chi	Psi	Omega
Ρ ρ	Σ σ	Τ τ	Υ υ	Φ φ	Χ χ	Ψ ψ	Ω ω
100	200	300	400	500	600	700	800

Digamma	Stigma	Koppa	Sampi
Ϝ	Ϛ	Ϙ	ϡ
6	6	90	900

Figure 68 Greek Alphabetic number system with Phoenician symbols below

Chapter 10. Egyptian and Greek mathematics

The second and later system is referred to as the alphabetic number system, and it used 24 Greek letters and 3 Phoenician ones to represent the numbers from one to ten, the tens from 10 to 90, and the hundreds from 100 to 900. In some cases X was apparently also used for 10 rather than Iota, and there are some variations in the letters used. Rather than being similar to the Hieroglyphic number system, this is similar to the Heiratic Egyptian system which had separate number signs for 1,2,3... 10, 20, 30... and so on. In this system, with reference to the table of letters above [Figure 68] the signs above [Figure 67] would represent 539. Often a line was added over the whole number to show that it was not a letter, as the same signs were used for writing and for numbers, something that could, and still can, at times be confusing.

Figure 69 Hieroglyphic sign for hekat grain measure (about 5 litres)

Just like Egyptian fractions, Greek fractions were Unit Fractions. They could not express fractions as multiples of smaller fractions, i.e. with a numerator such as with 5/7ths, and they had to be built up from the available unit fractions, yet never using the same one twice. This strange requirement may have been a hangover from the first simple fraction system that developed in Egypt, which is referred to as the Eye of Horus fraction system, and which was used solely for grain measurement (Gillings 1982: 210). With this system, the well known symbol of the eye of Horus was considered to be a compound symbol made up of several separate lines, each one of which represented a fraction of the whole [Figure 70].

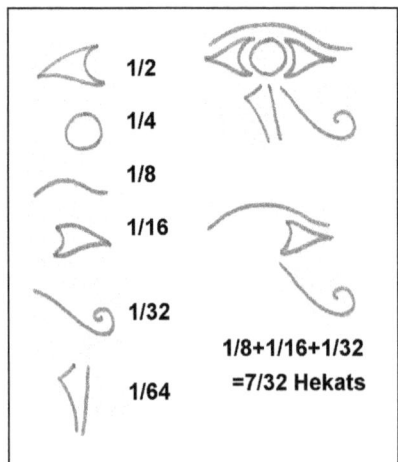

Figure 70 Horus Eye Fractions: Individual parts and example

The eye symbol was subdivided into 6 separate pieces, and these pieces represented ½, ¼, 1/8, 1/16, 1/32 and 1/64 respectively. In this way 37/64ths, for example, would be represented by drawing only the parts of the eye that represented ½, 1/16 and 1/64, as these add together to give 37/64ths. This fraction was not an abstract number, however, but a quantity of the dry measure for barley, wheat, corn and grain known as the 'hekat' [Figure 69]. The hekat was one thirtieth of a 'cubic cubit', which is 4.78 litres, and so dividing this with the Horus eye fractions into 64ths meant that measures as small as 0.074 litres, or 74ml could be expressed and differentiated. This is about 5 modern tablespoons of grain by volume. When dealing with grain in bulk, or for every day food measurement and distribution, this is an acceptably accurate system of measurement.

Nevertheless, an even smaller subdivision of volume was available known as the Ro, which was a 5th of the smallest subdivision of hekats, 1/64thm, and so was roughly equivalent to today's tablespoon by volume. The Ro fractions were shown as a mouth with the number of subdivisions scored out below it, or above it, and this is also what is seen used for the subdivisions of individual digits on the royal cubits [Figure 11]., and in Hieroglyphic writing in murals and temple inscriptions, as opposed to Hieratic fractions [Figure 71].

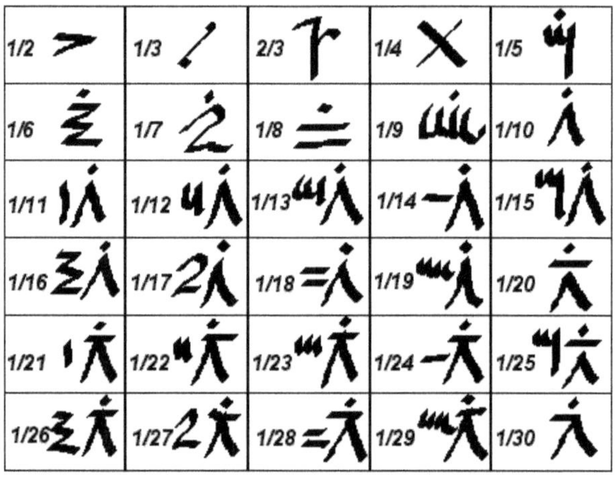

Figure 71 Basic Egyptian Hieratic unit fraction system

With the full unit fraction system that possibly developed from this earlier Horus Fraction system, other unit fractions were developed that were not based on subdivisions by twos, such as 1/3rds and $1/5^{th}$ and so on. Furthermore, much more complex and detailed subdivisions of numbers were attempted, and the complex unit fractions that evolved through this process were tabulated in their hundreds.

With the Unit Fraction system it was impossible, to take one example, to express what the product of dividing 2 by 7 was with a single number. For us this is $2/7^{th}$, but this could not be expressed as it was not a unit fraction, and it could also not be expressed as $1/7^{th}$ + 1/7ths, possibly due to the precursor Horus system whereby larger fractional

Chapter 10.   Egyptian and Greek mathematics

values were built up from smaller unit fractions in a progressively increasing sequences. For them, 2/7th would therefore be expressed as 1/4 + 1/28, and the Egyptian scribes developed endless tables of these complicated breakdowns to save time when performing calculations. The exception to this rule whereby only unit fractions could be expressed was the fraction 2/3, which had its own symbol. It is not clear why this was the case. In Hieratic shorthand, a unit fraction was generally differentiated from a simple whole number by a dot above the numerical symbol, so that, for example, 1/30th was shown as the whole number 30 with a single dot above it [Figure 71].

The Egyptians compiled lengthy tables of numbers broken down into unit fractions, such as a tables for 2 divided by all the odd numbers, from 3,5,7 etc, up to 101 (Gillings 1982: 50). The unit fractions thus derived could be extremely complex, for example 2 divided by 99 was 1/66 plus 1/198. At times several different breakdowns could be available, and the systematic procedures through which the Scribe chose one breakdown in preference to another are still being researched.

One of the breakdowns for 2 divided by 3 is as follows [Figure 72]:

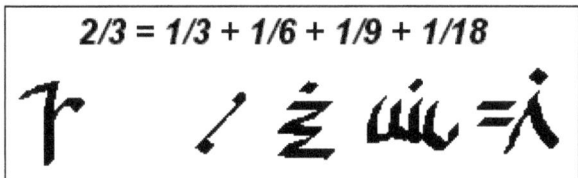

Figure 72 Typical Hieratic unit fraction break down

The breakdown shows that $2/3 = 1/3+1/6+1/9+1/18^{th}$, when expressed in unit fractions. As the Egyptians had a separate unique symbol just for 2/3, shown on the left in the figure, they would not have actually used this breakdown on a daily basis, but it demonstrates a possible example of what they could have done.

Likewise, the Greek alphabetic unit fraction system used dashes above whole numbers to indicate fractions, so that if B is 2, one half is shown as B". The example below [Figure 73] shows an alphabetic number solution to a division of 39 by 12, which is 3 + ¼ + 1/12.

$$\bar{\gamma}\ \delta''\ \iota\beta''$$

Figure 73 Greek alphabetic number 3+1/4+1/12

In this case the 3, represented by the y shaped 'gamma', is shown to be a whole number by way of a line above it. The delta represents four which is shown to be the unit fraction ¼ by way of the double dash above it, while the 12 is represented by iB, where i is 10 and B is 2, and this is shown to be the unit fraction $1/12^{th}$ by way of the double dash above both numbers together giving iB" [Figure 73].

For the mathematical historian today there is very little left to work from between the Rhind and Moscow Papyri from c.a. 1650 B.C. and the demotic mathematical papyri of the late period, which are roughly contemporary with the compilation of Euclid's Elements between 500 and 300 B.C. (Parker 1972).

In fact, other than a handful of minor texts, there is effectively a lacuna in the mathematical textual records of more than a millennium in length, and this needs to be explained, particularly when the period was notable for some of the most elaborate construction projects seen from Ancient Egypt. The Temple of Karnak, the Great Temple of Seti I at Abydos and Abu Simbel are just some of the construction projects that were carried out during that period, for which no construction calculations or documentation survive at all.

It is quite clear that many mathematical papyri must have existed at the time, and so we have to look at the plausible reasons for why they have not survived in greater numbers. The most straightforward answers relate to the durability of papyrus as a material. While it is an excellent lightweight and portable medium for recording large volumes of information, it is susceptible to destruction due to exposure to water, fire and even sunlight. While it can survive in good condition in the shaded dry conditions that could be found in an Egyptian temple for example, unique events involving water and in particular fire could play havoc with any archive, no matter how valuable.

Individual events that could bring about this sort of disaster could be, for example, flash floods, excessive inundations, fires started by accident or deliberately by disgruntled priests, scribes or commoners.

One of the major destruction events related to the temples in Upper Egypt was the invasion of Egypt by the Assyrians that took place in 671 B.C., and the Sack of Thebes that followed in 663 B.C. This was a great disaster for the Egyptians who had struggled against the Assyrians, albeit from under southern Kushite rule, for so many years.

It was during these struggles that the Egyptians had first grown closer to the Greeks who fought alongside them as mercenaries against the Assyrians on the Levant. After invading Egypt in 671 B.C. the Great Assyrian King Ashurbanipal set up the pharaoh Necho I as his vassal in Lower Egypt, and it was his nephew who returned in 663 B.C. to crush the Upper Egyptian city of Thebes with its great temples. Although Egypt recovered during the Saite period under the rule of the largely independent Psammetichus I, and then under the wise rule of Amasis

Chapter 10. Egyptian and Greek mathematics

II, it finally fell to the Persians in 525 B.C. at the Battle of Pelusium. After this disaster, the dangerously unstable Perisan Cambysus, son of Cyrus, wrecked the temples of Egypt and insulted the Egyptian religion by desecrating the burials of the pharaohs. Not until Alexander the Great defeated the Persians and arrived in Egypt in 332 B.C. could the ancient civilisation recover a semblance of its former glory again, but by then it would be from under Macedonian Greek rule.

When Alexander the Great and his armies conquered Egypt in 332 B.C. they set in motion a new movement that led to the creation of a new centre of learning with the ambitious objective of bringing together every text that had ever been produced in the entire world. It is documented that the Library of Alexandria actively collected written works from many regions, and it is possible that the new librarians brought any surviving archives from the temples of Thebes and Heliopolis and elsewhere in Egypt to the new establishment. Collecting together the surviving texts from the record halls in the temples, which were called 'The House of Life', Per-Ankhs, may have seemed a wise move that could help consolidate power and knowledge in one new centre, but if this sort of assimilation of material did happen, the decision was a poor one, as the Alexandrian library was destroyed in c.a. 48 B.C. when the Roman Empire arrived in Egypt with a bang. A naval power struggle between Caesar and Pompey spilled over into the port of Alexandria, and the library with its massive collection of ancient texts caught fire and was lost to the world forever. Over the next few centuries the Romans, completed the destructive work started by the Assyrians and Persians, and finally brought Old Egypt to its knees.

Although the Ancient Egyptian culture struggled on, the last remnants of the library, along with the Pagan religions of both the Greeks and the Egyptians, and the practice of writing in hieroglyphics, were finally stamped out altogether by the more extreme Christians, when the new religion took over the Roman Empire in the third and fourth centuries A.D.

Further more, once the ability to read hieratic, demotic and hieroglyphics had been lost to the world, the importance of the content of any surviving papyri would have been irrelevant. By the time that the Arabs were again establishing centres of learning in the east in the 8th to 10th centuries, and actively collecting copies of important works, any surviving papyri written in Hieratic, Demotic or Hieroglyphics would have been useless. Only the works produced in Greek could have been translated, and so this may explain why the famous texts that have survived are mostly those written in Alexandria and in the Greek colonies, in Greek. Over time any remnants of Egyptian mathematical texts would have deteriorated as they were written on papyrus, which was not a particularly durable material, as has been mentioned. It is interesting to note that of the surviving fragments, many have only come down to us due to their preservation as packaging paper from tombs and coffins.

These are just a few of the reasons why we had partly forgotten that mathematics and geometry came from Ancient Egypt, and this why the Rhind Mathematical Papyrus is so incredibly important. Its content must be properly analysed, synthesised and interpreted with respect to all of the archaeological and architectural evidence that is available. The interpretation of the architectural designs must also be carried out with meticulous thoroughness and attention to detail. Information regarding the origins of mathematics is contained within the very fabric of the buildings of Egypt, and only through careful archaeological survey of the buildings can this information be properly recovered.

One of the most important studies of this type that has already taken place was carried out by the Centre Franco-Égyptien pour l'étude des Temples de Karnak (Carlotti 1995). This study was able to derive historical information regarding the development of Egyptian measurement systems directly from the architecture. As well as identifying the precise values for the lengths of the cubits used in each phase of construction of various temples, Carlotti identified evidence for the 26th dynasty metrological reform that is thought to have taken place during the Saite period, and perhaps simultaneously with reforms of the canons of art used for drawing wall murals, and perhaps also the official adoption of Demotic as the script of preference. The metrological reforms had already been postulated in earlier works devoted to Egyptian canons of proportion and metrology (Iverson 1975; Robins 1994; Carlotti 1995: 129), but Carlotti's systematic collection of evidence from the different building phases and from different dynasties allowed an empirical comparison of the evidence to take place against the historical and theoretical backdrop.

Over the last few years I have been carrying out a related archaeological study regarding the situation on nearby Cyprus at this time. During the Saite Period Cyprus was very close to Egypt culturally as part of the new maritime trade network that was flourishing in the eastern Mediterranean. As has been noted, the military alliance between the Egyptians and Greeks and the burgeoning trade by sea that was developing across the region at the time mean that Cyprus and Egypt would have been in frequent contact. It is even reported by Herodotus that Cyprus was taken over by the Pharaoh Amasis II at the time, something that would have been expedient for a society under threat from the east that was losing ground on the mainland, and which wanted to maintain contact with the Greeks to the north, and access to Cyprus's resources of timber and copper.

The evidence I have collected from the architectural technology and funerary architecture from Iron Age Cyprus strongly suggests that the reformed system of measurement apparently instituted by the pharaonic rulers

Chapter 10. Egyptian and Greek mathematics

of Saite Egypt was widely used across the Eastern Mediterranean region including on the Levant and on Cyprus itself. This reformed cubit system consisted of a 6 palm rule of 533mm, which was subdivided into 24 digits. A surviving rod of this type was discovered by Petrie on the Levant at the start of the 20th century, and is now kept in the Petrie Museum in London.

Likewise in Egypt, the data derived from the columns and pylons of the various construction phases at Karnak suggest that by the reign of Osorkon I (900 B.C.) the old Egyptian royal cubit had already drifted or lengthened towards 0.533m, perhaps through repeated copying of rules and cumulative normal errors found on long lived construction sites. The data further suggests that by the reign of Taharqa (690 B.C.-664 B.C.) variations are seen in the architecture as long as 0.54m. This gradual lengthening seems to have first taken place during the late 18th, 19th and 20th dynasties (Carlotti 1995: 92), whereas before this the Egyptian cubit was much more consistent to its Old and Middle Kingdom value of 0.523/0.524m. Although this slight lengthening may have been a New Kingdom phenomenon, and may be indicative of less rigorously enforced standards or a less centralised society emerging towards the end of the New Kingdom, the official reform of the overall measure from 7 palms into 6 palms seems to have been a 26th dynasty Late Period event (Carlotti 1995: 129).

Figure 74 The antique 6-part 532mm cubit from the Petrie Museum in London

The photograph above shows the putative example of the Late Egyptian or 'reformed cubit' found on the Levant from the collection of the Petrie Museum in London, catalogue number UC-36148. It is shown beside a modern scale rule based on the Older 7 palm, 28-digit Egyptian cubit for comparison.

At this scale is only just possible to see that the lower rule is slightly longer than the modern royal cubit above it, but this difference is an important historical issue that enables us to observe historically relevant differences in standing architecture.

The architecture of Cyprus was influenced by all of the cultures that it was in contact with, including those on the Levant, on Asia Minor, from Greece and from Egypt, yet it seems as though it was the Egyptian systems that were adopted across the island.

All in all, the evidence from Egypt, the Levant and Greece suggests a great deal of continuity between the older Egyptian mathematical and geometrical systems and the younger Greek ones that were born out of them. The evidence is certainly incomplete, meaning that a full picture is difficult to piece together, so the priority must be to use the evidence that is already available more effectively.

The evidence that we do have such as the Late Egyptian Demotic Papyri, and Euclid's Elements, which was composed not long after the Demotic works were written, needs to be revisited and re-interpreted. This is particularly important when considered in light of the growing evidence of close contact between Greece and Egypt at the time the mathematical and architectural skills were first being transferred to Greece in the early Iron Age between c.a. 650 and 500 B.C.

Other aspects of Archaic Greek culture show clear evidence of Egyptian influence, in particular the earliest proportional statuary, known today in English as Kouros and Kore statues, which show clear evidence of Egyptian artistic techniques. These statues are important with respect to understanding the history of measurement techniques, as the earliest Greek methods were closely linked to the dimensions and proportions of parts of the body.

This effectively concludes this general level review of some of the major issues in the history of Greco-Egyptian mathematics that may need to be revisited in more detail. As this is an appendix, however, it is worth digressing briefly to look at a subject matter that brings together several of the historical issues we have been looking at, including the life of Alexander the Great, the cartouche and shen symbols and the recovery of hieroglyphics during the 19th century.

While we have been looking at the debt that Greek culture owed to Ancient Egypt, it was in fact the Aegean Greeks, or more specifically, the Macedonians, who saved Egypt from the oppressive rule of a foreign occupying power in 332 B.C. Alexander the Great and his army overthrew the oppressive rule of the Persians across the Middle East at this time, and he was welcomed into Egypt as a saviour, not as a foreign invader. He was crowned as the reincarnation of Amun-Re, and as the fully legitimate pharaoh of the sacred land of Egypt.

As pharaoh, his name was protected within the royal cartouche of Egypt.

2,200 years later, in the early 19th century, the hieroglyphic text spelling out Alexander's name was found within these cartouches and very aptly became one of the first of those translated by Champollion, Young and others, when they finally managed to decipher hieroglyphics once more. The name of Alexander, the saviour of Egypt, served to aid in the recovery of hieroglyphics in part because it had been protected by the cartouche symbol, and had therefore been identified as a royal name by the scholars.

The name of Alexander's favourite general Ptolemy, and his descendents who also carried that name as pharaohs

Chapter 10. Egyptian and Greek mathematics

of Egypt, was another of the first few names translated.

Alexander's name is shown below in the photograph from a temple wall in Thebes [Figure 75], and shows, from top to bottom, the bird sign for A, the lion for L, the libation bowl for K, an S, a Y to the right side which is the feather, an N which is the zigzag, a hand which is the D, the mouth sign which is the same as that used for the Ro fractions, representing R, and a final S again. This spells out 'ALKSYNDRS', which is phonetically pronounced in a very similar way to ALEXANDER in English. In many Middle Eastern countries there are also cities named after Alexander, but these are often called 'ISKANDER', which also continues to be the form used for the personal name in many regions. The true pronunciation of his name probably lies somewhere between these different forms, and given the existence of a final S in the Hieroglyphic version, the correct form was perhaps very close to the modern Greek version ALEKSANDROS.

The modern word for the pharaonic symbol 'cartouche' also has an interesting history that is worth expanding on. As was mentioned earlier, the use of the word cartouche in association with the Egyptian royal names was probably derived from the time of Napoleon's expedition into Egypt at the end of the 18th century. The word was used for the gun cartridges or cartouches that Napoleon's soldiers carried with them, and it is widely thought that the similarity in shapes between the cartridges and the pharaonic symbols led to the same word being used for both. The word cartouche is ultimately derived from the Italian *cartoccio*, meaning a paper (*cart*) bag twisted into a little packet shape, usually for cooking small vegetables or spaghetti, and in fact there is a visible similarity between the two shapes. Gun cartridges were originally made up as little 'cartridge paper' containers, with the lead balls included in the packet along with the powder charge, so that they resembled small Christmas 'crackers'.

Figure 75 Cartouche of Alexander the Great from temple wall in Thebes

Like the word 'cartouche' in French, the English word 'cartridge', refers to this cylindrical paper or flannel container (and later metal casing) for holding a complete charge of powder, and often also the bullet or the shot, for a rifle, machine gun, or other small arm [Figure 76]. Duckers writes: "Composed of stiff paper (hence 'cartridge paper') and holding a measured charge of powder and a lead ball, cartridges could be made by soldiers in their spare time. The soldier bit the end off and poured first the powder and then the ball into the barrel, using the ramrod to push down the paper tube as wadding to stop the contents falling out of the barrel. When the musket was fired, the wadding burned and fouled the barrel. Not until the invention of breech loaders did cartridges significantly alter in look, with the eventual introduction of metal cartridge cases for the Snider rifle" (Duckers 2005: 8). In England, the word cartouche was in fact used, but referred to canvas shoulder bags with leather bottoms and a buttoned flap in which the larger cartridges for field artillery were packed, stored and transported (Franklin 2008: 85).

Figure 76 Replicas of early cartridges with lead balls and a 'cartoccio' food packet

Yet another use of the word is from Italian art, and in that case it refers to either an artistic device containing the names of people, included on paintings or in a separate plaque attached to a painting, or in architecture when a rounded, convex surface surrounded with carved ornamental scrollwork is installed on a wall for receiving a painted or low-relief decoration.

We know that Napoleon took artists, architects and scholars with him to Egypt as well as solders, so it seems possible that one of his 'savants' with a knowledge of Italian art was the first to have used the word with reference to its Italian meaning and its function of containing proper names, only for the military people to connect it to the shape of the paper containers that they were making up, and firing, on a daily basis.

Understanding that the hieroglyphic cartouches contained names was one of the earliest breakthroughs made in the decipherment of hieroglyphics.

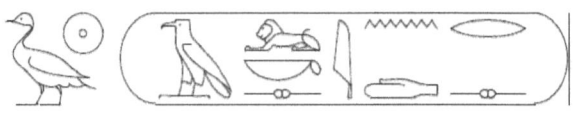

Figure 77 Transcribed glyphs spelling 'Sah Ra' (son of Ra) and ALKSYNDRS

Chapter 10. Egyptian and Greek mathematics

This concludes the appendix on the general history of Greco-Egyptian mathematics and associated historical events. Returning to the main topic of this chapter, the recovery of Egyptian mathematics over the last 150 years has been a slow but steady process, and is one that continues to this day. Further assimilation, synthesis, analysis and interpretation of the architectural and textual evidence should certainly be pursued, and the results of this could be extensive. Based on the evidence that is already available, it is clear that Egyptian mathematical capabilities extended a long way beyond what is demonstrated on the handful of papyri that have survived. There is also clear evidence that the relationship between Greco-Egyptian and Egyptian mathematics, such as between Euclid's Elements which was compiled in Alexandria and the Demotic Mathematical Papyri that preceded it was much closer than has been acknowledged by text focussed mathematical historians. In fact, in light of the new evidence becoming available, we need to treat the statements made by the Greeks themselves, when they acknowledged their debt to the Ancient Egyptians, with the seriousness they deserve, instead of trying to explain them away based on text focussed critical methods that have no relevance to the real history of the region. The quotes from the Greeks are reviews in the final appendix that follows.

Egyptologist Dr Margaret Alice Murray (Murray 1963: 314), a close friend and pupil of Flinders Petrie, was already pushing for these reforms to the traditional narrative in her study of Egyptian culture in 1963. She wrote the following paragraph, which is closely related to the themes of this chapter and so is quoted here in full. It was included in a short section at the back of her book devoted to the life of the Late Flinders Petrie: "In 1877 there appeared a little book of rather more than a hundred and fifty pages called *Inductive Metrology*. The author was a young man of four and twenty, who signed himself W. M. Flinders Petrie. The publication of that modest volume transformed the whole of the study of the Past and brought its author with a rush to the forefront of the learned world. Until Petrie's appearance in the field there had been no archaeology, only antiquarianism, with collections of 'curios', or 'relics from the past'. And it was the hobby of a few learned men, whose horizon was bounded by Biblical or Classical history. They were the slaves of the written word, and believed nothing that was not vouched for by documentary evidence. But even documents were not always above suspicion if they did not agree with preconceived ideas, and Herodotus's accounts of were treated with scorn. It was considered clever to say of Herodotus "Father of History, Indeed! Father of Lies more likely!" To these people Greek Art was a sacred thing, which had come into the world full-blown. Greek literature also had no beginning. They were not quite separate and special creations of God, but were very nearly so, and it was almost blasphemy to suggest that when the Greeks themselves said how much they owed to Egypt they might in fact have been speaking the truth."

As the archaeological evidence uncovered over the years has demonstrated time and time again, Herodotus was indeed generally speaking the truth when he described as best he could the things he had seen and the people he had met and talked with on his travels to Egypt. In her turn, it seems that Dr Margaret Murray was also quite correct to trust Herodotus and his statements.

A re-assessment of the mathematical capabilities of the Ancient Egyptian is clearly now required, and by extension, the origins of Greco-Egyptian and Greek mathematics. This is demanded by the new conclusions derived here from archaeological, architectural and historical evidence, and it was the intention of this work to encourage this re-evaluation as far as possible.

11. Appendix 4: Quotes from the Greeks

Below are just some of the quotes from antiquity where the Greeks give due credit to the Egyptians for providing the foundations of their mathematics, scholarship and other aspects of their civilisation:

"Thus the mathematical sciences originated in the neighbourhood of Egypt, because there the priestly class was allowed leisure" (Aristotle, Metaphysics I.I.15, 1, trans. by H. Tredennick).

"On a visit to Egypt [Pythagoras] became a student of the religion of the people, and was first to bring to the Greeks all philosophy" (Isocrates, Busiris 27-30).

"...geometry was invented, it is said, from the measurement of lands which is made necessary by the Nile when it confounds the boundaries at the time of its overflows. This science, then, is believed to have come to the Greeks from the Aegyptians; astronomy and arithmetic from the Phoenicians; and at present the far the greatest store of knowledge in every other branch of philosophy is had from these cities. And if one must believe Poseidonius, the ancient dogma about atoms originated with Mochus, a Sidonian [Phoenician], born before the Trojan times" (Strabo, Geography, 16, 2, trans. by H. L. Jones).

"...Egyptians have not only been accepted by the present inhabitants but have aroused no little admiration among the Greeks; and for that reason those men who have won the greatest repute in intellectual things have been eager to visit Egypt in order to acquaint themselves with its laws and institutions.... [Egypt] was nevertheless eagerly visited by Orpheus and the poet Homer in the earliest times and in later times by many others, such as Pythagoras of Samos and Solon the lawgiver" (Diodorus Siculus, Book I. 68).

"[Pythagoras] left the city and went off to Egypt and Babylon, to satisfy his fondness for learning..." (Strabo, Geography 14. I. 16, trans. by H.L. Jones)

"[Thales] exhorted [Pythagoras] to sail into Egypt, and associate with the Memphian and Diosolitan priests. For he confessed that his own reputation for wisdom, was derived from the instructions of these priests; but that he was neither naturally, nor by exercise, endued with those excellent prerogatives, which were so visibly displayed in the person of Pythagoras. Thales, therefore, gladly announced to him, from all these circumstances, that he would become the wisest and most divine of all men, if he associated with these Egyptian priests" (Iamblichus, Life of Pythagoras, Chapter II).

"This is also confirmed by the most learned of Greeks such as Solon, Thales, Plato, Eudoxus, Pythagoras, and as some say, even Lycurgus going to Egypt and conversing with the priests; of whom they say Euxodus was a hearer of Chonuphis of Memphis, Solon of Sonchis of Sais, and Pythagoras of Oenuphis of Heliopolis. Wherefore the last named, being, as is probable, more than ordinarily admired by the men, and they also by him imitated their symbolic and mysterious way of talking; obscuring his sentiments with dark riddles. For the greatest part of Pythagoric precepts fall nothing short of those sacred writings they call hieroglyphical..." (Plutarch, Morals, 10)

"He [Pythagoras] had three silver flagons made and took them as presents to each of the priests of Egypt ... While still young, so eager was he for knowledge, he left his own country ... he learnt the Egyptian language, so we learn from Antiphon in his book On Men of Outstanding Merit, and he also journeyed among the Chaldeans and Magi" (Diogenes Laertius, VIII. 2-4).

"Besides these which have been here mentioned, there are many other practices… which the Greeks have borrowed from Egypt " Herodotus, book II

And finally, although he is not Greek:

"If Egyptian multiplication was so clumsy and difficult, how did it come about that these same techniques were still being used in Coptic times, in Greek times, and even up to the Byzantine period, a thousand or more years later? No nation, over a period of more than a millennium, was able to improve on the Egyptian notation and methods. The fact is that, despite their notation, the scribes were in fact quite skilful in devising ingenious methods of attack on algebraic and geometric problems as well, so that their successors remained content with what came down to them" (Gillings 1982: 16)

12. References

Adkins, L. A., R.
2001 *The Keys of Egypt: The Race to Crack the Hieroglyph Code.* Harper Perennial

Allen, J. P.
2001 *Middle Egyptian, An Introduction to the Language and Culture of Hieroglyphs.* Cambridge: Cambridge University Press.

Arnold, B.
1990 The Past as Propaganda: Totalitarian Archaeology in Nazi Germany. *Antiquity* 64: 464-78.

Arnold, D.
1991 *Building in Egypt: Pharaonic Stone Masonry.* Oxford: Oxford University Press.

2005 The Royal Cult Complexes of the Old and Middle Kingdoms. in *Temples of Ancient Egypt.* B. E. Schafer ed. Cairo: The American University in Cairo Press.

Baines, J. and J. Malek
1980 *Atlas of Ancient Egypt (Cultural Atlas).* New York: Facts on File Inc.

Bernal, M.
1987 *Black Athena : The Afroasiatic Roots of Classical Civilization.* London: Free Association Books.

2001 *Black Athena Writes Back: Martin Bernal Responds to his Critics.* London: Duke University Press.

Betancourt, P. P.
1977 *The Aeolic Style in Architecture: A Survey of its Development in Palestine, the Halikarnassos Peninsula, and Greece, 1000-500 B.C.* Princeton: Princeton University Press.

Bey, M.
1878 Le système métrique actuel d'Égypte. *Journal Asiatique* Septieme Serie(Tome Premier): 67-110.

Boas, R. P.
1979 Award for Distinguished Service to Otto Neugebauer. *American Mathematics Monthly* 86(2): 77-78.

Brock, J. F.
2005 Four Surveyors of the Gods In the XVIII Dynasty of Egypt - New Kingdom c. 1400 B.C. *The Proceedings of the Working Week 2005 of the International Federation of Surveyors (FIG). (available online).*

Cajori, F.
1930 Reviewed Work(s): The Rhind Mathematical Papyrus. by A.B.Chace; H.P. Manning; R.C. Archibald; L.Bull. *The American Mathematical Monthly* 37(4): 189-191.

Carlotti, J. F.
1995 Contribution à l'étude métrologique de quelques monuments du temple d'Amon-Rê à Karnak. *Cahiers de Karnak X,*: 65-139.

Chace, A. B.
1929 *The Rhind Mathematical Papyrus.* Ohio: Oberlin.

Chrisomalis, S.
2003 The Egyptian Origin of Greek Alphabetic Numerals. *Antiquity* 77(297): 485-497.

Clarke, S. and R. Engelbach
1991 *Ancient Egyptian Construction and Architecture* Dover Publications.

Chapter 12.   References

Cole, J. H.
  1925 *The Determination of the Exact Size and Orientation of the Great Pyramid of Giza. Paper no 39*. Cairo: Survey of Egypt.

Curl, J. S.
  1994 *Egyptomania : the Egyptian revival : a recurring theme in the history of taste*. Manchester: Manchester University Press.

Davis, T. D.
  2004 *Shifting Sands: The Rise and Fall of Biblical Archaeology* Oxford University Press.

Dekoulakou-Sideris, I.
  1990 A metrological relief from Salamis. *American Journal of Archaeology*. 94: 445-451.

Dilke, O. A. W.
  1987 *Reading the Past: Mathematics and Measurement*. London: British Museum Publications.

Dorner, J.
  1991 *Mitteilungen des Deutschen Archäologischen Instituts, Abteilung Kairo* 47.

Drower, M. S.
  1985 *Flinders Petrie: A Life in Archaeology*. London: Victor Gollancz Ltd.

Duckers, P.
  2005 *British Military Rifles 1800-2000*. Princes Risborough: Shire Books.

Ebeling, E. and B. Meissner
  1999 Masse und Gewichte. *Reallexikon Der Assyriologie: Unter Mitwirkung Zahlreicher Fachgelehrter*. Berlin and New York: . De Gruyter. 457-530.

Edwards, I. E. S.
  1979 *The Pyramids of Egypt*. Middlesex: Penguin.

Emery, W. B.
  1991 *Archaic Egypt. Culture and Civilisation in Egypt 5000 years ago*. London: Penguin.

Firth, C. M., J. E. Quibell, et al.
  1935 *Excavations at Saqqara : The Step Pyramid*. Cairo.

Franklin, C. E.
  2008 *British Napoleonic Field Artillery*. Stroud: Spellmount.

Gardner, M.
  1957 *Fads and Fallacies in the Name of Science*. New York: Dover Publications.

Gillings, R. J.
  1982 *Mathematics in the Time of the Pharaohs*. New Yrok: Dover.

Griffith, F. L.
  1901 Chronological Value of Egyptian Words Found in the Bible. *Proceedings of the Society of Biblical Archaeology* 23: 72-77.

Hale, C.
  2004 *Himmler's Crusade. The True Story of the 1938 Nazi Expedition into Tibet*. London: Bantam.

Herodotus.
  1996 *Histories*. Hertfordshire: Wordsworth Classics.

Herz-Fischler, R.
  2000 *The Shape of the Great Pyramid*. Ontario: Wilfred Laurier University Press.

Chapter 12. References

Hollenback, G. M.
1997 The Myth of Egyptian Pi. *Skeptic* 5(4).

Home, R.
2006 Scientific Survey and Land Settlement in British Colonialism, with Particular Reference to Land Tenure Reform in the Middle East 1920-50. *Planning Perspectives* 21: 1-22.

Hornung, E.
1999 *The Ancient Egyptian Books of the Afterlife (trans. David Lorton)* Cornell University Press.

Imhausen, A.
2003 *Ägyptische Algorithmen. Eine Untersuchungzu den mittelägyptischen mathematischen Aufgabentexten.* Wiesbaden: Harrassowitz.

Ioppolo, G.
1967 La tavola delle unita di misura nel mercato augusteo di Leptis Magna. *Quad A Libya* 5: 89-98.

Iverson, E.
1975 *Canon and Proportion in Egyptian Art.* Warminster: Aris and Phillips Ltd.

Jacobson, D. and F. Cobbing
2005 "A Record of Discovery and Adventure". Claude Reignier Conder's Contributions to the Exploration of Palestine. *Near Eastern Archaeology* 68(4): 166-179.

Jordan, P.
2006 Esoteric Egypt. in *Archaeological Fantasies. How Pseudoarchaeology Misrepresents the Past and Misleads the Public*. G. G. Fagan ed. Routledge: 109-128.

Karabell, Z.
2004 *Parting the Desert. The Creation of the Suez Canal.* London: John Murray.

Kemp, B.
2005 *Ancient Egypt. Anatomy of a Civilisation.* Oxford: Routledge.

Lacau, P. and H. Chevrier
1969 *Une Chapelle de Sesostris 1er à Karnak.* Cairo: Service des Antiquities.

Lamy, L.
1991 *New Light on Ancient Knowledge: Egyptian Mysteries.* London: Thames and Hudson.

Larkin, M.
1999 Newsbriefs: Earliest Egyptian Glyphs. *Archaeology* 52(2).

Lauer, J. P.
1931 Étude sur Quelques Monuments de la IIIe Dynastie (Pyramide à Degrés de Saqqarah). *Annales du Service des Antiquites de L'Egypte, IFAO* 31: 60.

1960 Observations sur les Pyramides. *le Caire: Imprimerie de l'Institut Français d'Archéologie Orientale.*

1974 *Le Mystère des Pyramides* Paris: Presse de la cité.

1976 *Saqqara. The Royal Cemetery of Memphis.* London: Thames and Hudsom.

Lefkowitz, M. R.
2000 The Ancient World As Seen By Afrocentrists. in *Afrocentrismes: L'histoire des Africains entre Égypte et Amérique* F. X. Fauvelle-Aymar, J. P. Chrétien and C. H. Perrot ed. Paris: Karthala: 229-48.

2008 *History Lesson: A Race Odyssey* Yale University Press

Chapter 12.   References

Legon, J. A. R.
1979 The Plan of the Giza Pyramids. *Archaeological Reports of the Archaeology Society of Staten Island* 10(1).

1988 A Ground Plan at Giza. *Discussions in Egyptology* 10: 33-40.

1989 The Giza Ground Plan and Sphinx. *Discussions in Egyptology* 14: 53-60.

1990 The 14 to 11 proportion at Meydum. *Discussions in Egyptology* 17: 15-22.

1991 The Giza Site Plan Revisited. *Göttinger Miszellen* 124: 69-78.

1991 On Pyramid Dimensions and Proportions. *Discussions in Egyptology* 20: 35-44.

Lehner, M.
1997 *The Complete Pyramids*. London: Thames & Hudson Ltd

Lepsius, R. C.
2000 *The Ancient Cubit and its Subdivisions. Expanded and Edited my Michael St. John.* London: Museum Bookshop Publications.

Lichtheim, M.
2006 *Ancient Egyptian Literature: New Kingdom 2:* University of California Press.

Lightbody, D.
2008 The Cubit in Iron Age Cypriot Architecture. *Report of the Department of Antiquities, Cyprus.*

Livio, M.
2002 *The Golden Ratio*. London: Headline Book Publishing.

Lutley, K. and J. Bunbury
2008 The Nile on the Move. *Egyptian Archaeology* 32.

MacHaffie, B. Z.
1981 Monumental Facts and Higher Critical Fancies": Archaeology and the Popularisation of Old Testament Criticism in Nineteenth Century Britian. *Church History* 50: 316.

Maragioglio, V. and C. A. Rinaldi
1964 *L'Architettura delle Piramidi Menfite IV:* Rapallo.

Marchand, S. L.
1996 *Down From Olympus : Archaeology and Philhellenism in Germany, 1750-1970*. Princeton, N.J.: Princeton University Press.

Mendelsshon, K.
1974 *The Riddle of the Pyramids* Thames and Hudson.

Mojsov, B.
2005 *Osiris*. London: Blackwell Publishing.

Morris, I.
1994 Archaeologies of Greece. in *Classical Greece. Ancient Histories and Modern Archaeologies*. I. Morris ed. Cambridge University Press: 8-47.

Moscrop, J. J.
2000 *Measuring Jerusalem : the Palestine Exploration Fund and British interests in the Holy Land*. London: Leicester University Press.

Murray, M. A.
1963 *The Splendour that was Egypt. A general survey of Egyptian culture and civilisation*. London: Sidgwick and Jackson Limited.

Chapter 12.   References

Neugebauer, O.
1969 *The Exact Sciences in Antiquity*. New York: Dover.

Palter, R.
1996 Black Athena, Afrocentrism and the History of Science. in *Black Athena Revisited*. M. R. Lefkowitz and G. MacLean Rogers ed. Chapel Hill, N.C: UNC Press.

Parker, R. A.
1972 *Demotic Mathematical Papyrii*. Rhode Island: Brown University Press.

Petit, T.
2000 Usage de la coudée dans l'architecture palatiale de Chypre au premier millénaire. *Ktema* 23: 173-189.

Petrie, W. M. F.
1883 *The Pyramids and Temples of Gizeh*. London: Field & Tuer.

1886-1888 *Naukratis*. London Trübner.

1892 *Medum*. London: David Nutt, 270, 271, Strand.

1912 *Egypt and Israel*. London: Society for promoting Christian knowledge.

1926 *Ancient Weights and Measures*. London: Department of Egyptology University College.

1931 *Seventy Years in Archaeology*. London: Sampson Low Marston & Co.

1940 *Wisdom of the Egyptians*. London: British School of Archaeology in Egypt and B. Quaritch Ltd.

Quirke, S.
2001 *The Cult of Ra. Sun Worship in Ancient Egypt from the Pyramids to Cleopatra*. London: Thames & Hudson Ltd.

Reisenauer, E. M.
2003 "The Battle of the Standards": Great Pyramid metrology and the British identity 1859-1890. *The Historian* 65.

Rihill, T. E.
1999 *Greek Science*. Oxford: Oxford University Press.

Robins, G.
1994 *Proportion and Style in Ancient Egyptian Art*. Austin: University of Texas Press.

Robins, G. and C. Schute
1990 Irrational Numbers and Pyramids. *Discussions in Egyptology* 18: 43-53.

Romer, J.
2007 *The Great Pyramid: Ancient Egypt Revisited* Cambridge University Press.

Rossi, C.
1999 Note on the Pyramidion found at Dahshur. *Journal of Egyptian Archaeology* 85: 219-222.

2003 *Architecture and Mathematics in Ancient Egypt*. Cambridge: University Press.

Sayce, A. H.
1890 *Fresh Light from the Ancient Monuments*. London: The Religious Tract Society.

1894 *The "Higher Criticism" and the Verdict of the Monuments*. London: Society for Promoting Christian Knowledge

Schafer, B. E.
2005 *Temples of Ancient Egypt*. Cairo: The American University in Cairo press.

Schepler, H. C.
1950 The Chronology of Pi. *Mathematics Magazine* 23(3).

Chapter 12.   References

Scott, N. E.
  1942 Egyptian Cubit Rods. *The Metropolitan Museum of Art Bulletin, New Series,* Vol. 1(No. 1): pp. 70-75.

Shiloh, Y.
  1979 The Proto-Aeolic Capital and Israelite Ashlar Masonry. *QEDEM Monographs of the Institute of Archaeology.* Jerusalem. The Hebrew University.

Silberman, N. A.
  1998 The Sea Peoples, the Victorians, and Us: Modern Social Ideology and Changing Archaeological Interpretations of the Late Bronze Age Collapse. in *Mediterranean Peoples in Transition: Thirteenth to Early Tenth Centuries BCE.* S. Gitin, A. Amazar and E. Stern ed. Jerusalem: Israeli Exploration Society: 268-275.

Smith, C. B.
  2004 *How The Great Pyramid was Built.* Washington D.C.: Smithsonian Books.

Smyth, C. P.
  1880 *Our Inheritance in the Great pyramid.* London: W. Isbister.

Spencer, A. J.
  1979 *Brick Architecture in Ancient Egypt.* Warminster: Aris and Phillips.

St. John, M.
  2000 *Three Cubits Compared.* London: The Museum Bookshop Ltd.

Taylor, J.
  1859 *The Great Pyramid: Why was it Built? And Who Built it?* London.

Tod, M. N.
  1950 The Alphabetic Numeral System in Attica. *Annual of the British School at Athens* 45: 126-139.

Tompkins, P.
  1971 *Secrets of the Great Pyramid.* New York: Harpers and Row.

Verner, M.
  2003 *The Pyramids: Their Archaeology and History.* London: Atlantic Books.

Wheeler, M.
  1935 Pyramids and their Purpose. *Antiquity* 9: 161-189.

  1953 Adventure and Flinders Petrie. *Antiquity* 27.

Wilkinson, R. H.
  1999 *Symbol and Magic in Egyptian Art.* New York: Thames and Hudson.

  2000 *The Complete Temples of Ancient Egypt.* London: Thames & Hudson Ltd.

  2003 *Reading Egyptian Art. A Hieroglyphic Guid to Ancient Egyptian Painting and Sculpture.* London: Thames and Hudson Ltd.

www.ingramcontent.com/pod-product-compliance
Lightning Source LLC
Chambersburg PA
CBHW061544010526
44113CB00023B/2795